Interdisciplinary Unit

Shakespeare

CHALLENGING

Illustrator:
Kathy Bruce

Editor:
Walter Kelly, M.A.

Editorial Project Manager:
Ina Massler Levin, M.A.

Editor-in-Chief:
Sharon Coan, M.S. Ed

Art Direction:
Elayne Roberts

Product Manager:
Phil Garcia

Imaging:
Alfred Lau

Cover Artist:
Agi Palinay

Publishers:
Rachelle Cracchiolo, M.S. Ed.
Mary Dupuy Smith, M.S. Ed.

Author:

Mari Lu Robbins

Teacher Created Materials, Inc.
P.O. Box 1040
Huntington Beach, CA   92647
ISBN-1-55734-614-3

©1995 Teacher Created Materials, Inc.   Made in U.S.A.

Table of Contents

Table of Contents *(cont.)*

Introduction

Although 400 years have passed since William Shakespeare wrote his plays, they are alive and well in the world of theater and film today and loved by millions of people. This unit is designed for the busy English teacher who wants to share the richness of Shakespeare's work with students and relate that work to the world in which he lived, as well as the world of today. It contains activities across the curriculum to be used by the individual teacher or shared in team teaching with instructors of other disciplines around the basic theme of Shakespeare and his works.

This unit is filled with a wide variety of lesson ideas and reproducible pages designed for use with middle and junior high students. The core of the unit consists of three plays written by Shakespeare— one comedy, one history, and one tragedy—and several of his sonnets, as well as other poetry and writings, knowledge of which was considered to be the hallmark of an educated person during the Elizabethan period when Shakespeare was writing and producing his plays. Lessons which cross curriculum boundaries are provided to widen the students' grasp of life as it was for real people in Shakespeare's time, relating it to life today.

The plays have been carefully chosen for their current appropriateness of theme and content for adolescent students; they include *Much Ado About Nothing, Romeo and Juliet,* and *Richard III. Much Ado About Nothing* is a silly, romantic comedy with likeable characters and an evil villain. *Romeo and Juliet,* the world's most famous love story, is about two teenaged lovers who die tragically because of misunderstanding and miscommunication. *Richard III* is based on the story of a diabolically calculating prince who lies, manipulates, and kills his way to the throne of England. These plays contain some of Shakespeare's most beautiful poetry and most dramatic moments, and they illustrate his ability to reveal the souls of his characters to the audience through words and actions.

Why Interdisciplinary Teaching?

The world in which today's students live is rapidly changing, very diverse, and full of many challenging things for them to learn in a short time. Because of the complexity of modern life and the many distractions provided by the media and social pressures, many students have not acquired the necessary background to totally comprehend all that they read; nor have they learned how to consciously relate what they already know to what they are expected to learn.

Reading is a dynamic process which involves more than just looking at the printed page and taking meaning from it. The reader also puts meaning into what he or she reads while simultaneously taking meaning from it. What the reader already knows goes into the reading, so that there is a constant give-and-take between the reader and the material being read.

Interdisciplinary teaching provides a way to supply the missing links in the student's fund of knowledge, so that the student will be able to better comprehend what he or she reads. It also provides a format for helping the student to acquire new information which is relevant to what is being studied, as well as to what has already been learned.

Interdisciplinary teaching is a way of helping students make connections between what has been and what is and of helping them to see the connections among people, places, events, and ideas. In this way, interdisciplinary teaching helps students achieve a higher degree of mastery of a piece of literature than they otherwise would be able to do.

Introduction *(cont.)*

Why Shakespeare?

For 400 years, Shakespeare has been considered the greatest dramatist and poet in the English-speaking world. His plays are produced thousands of times each year in theaters all over the world, and audiences today are as enthralled as the ones who first attended them in London. His plays are filled with action, intrigue, mystery, rollicking humor, and heart-wrenching tragedy, sometimes all within the bounds of the same play. His plays are timeless.

The characters in Shakespeare's plays are complete in all varieties of human experience. Some of them are good people who make bad choices. Some are silly people who do not know they are silly. A few of them are monsters. Some are truly tragic people, good but with flaws in character which lead them to destruction. Some are lovers embracing life with a passion, and others are losers who spend their lives in anger and hate. They represent all the varieties of personality, motivation, and character which exist in humankind.

Shakespeare was a master of our complex English language, and he filled his plays with poetry and prose in a way unequaled by any other writer. He wrote with an incredible vocabulary of over 29,000 words, which is astounding when one considers that the King James Version of the Bible uses slightly over 3,000. Many of those words are used in sophisticated puns and wordplay, yet he wrote for the commoner, as well as for the educated. The language of Shakespeare is rich beyond that of any other writer.

When you communicate a love of Shakespeare to your students, you give them a gift they can enjoy the rest of their lives, a gift which will empower them to see the world in all its manifestations. And when you teach cooperatively with teachers of other disciplines around a common theme, you empower students by showing them how to make connections between themselves and others—in the past and in the present.

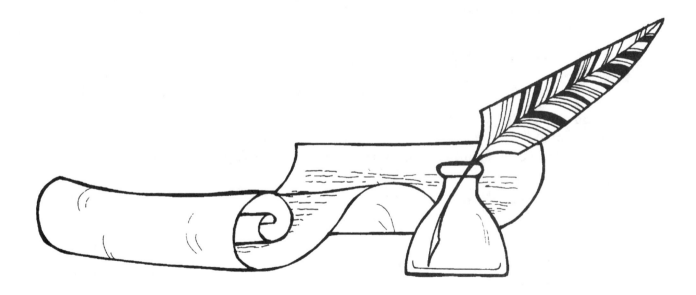

To keep this resource intact so it can be used year after year, you may wish to punch holes in the pages and store them in a three-ring binder.

Setting the Scene

Before beginning to read the first play, setting the scene in the classroom will help your students to gain the most from their reading and performing. The following are some suggestions for general things to do in the classroom.

❖ Display historical maps of England and London and discuss how London might be different today from the way it was four hundred years ago.

❖ Display posters of films, plays, or ballets made of or based on Shakespearean plays such as *Kiss Me Kate*, *West Side Story*, *Romeo and Juliet* and *A Midsummer Night's Dream*. Check with theater managers and local theater groups to obtain them.

❖ Display pictures of Elizabethan musical instruments.

❖ Display large pictures of Shakespeare, Stratford-upon-Avon, English royalty, the Globe Theatre, or any other aspect of Elizabethan life which you can find.

❖ Contact theater groups — ones which regularly produce Shakespearean plays and put on Shakespeare festivals — to request photos and posters for current or past productions.

❖ Plan and arrange a field trip to see a production or film of a Shakespearean play.

❖ Some Shakespearean companies regularly send out actors to present segments of their plays for school assemblies or drama classes. Check with nearby companies to learn whether they have traveling actors who will come to the school to give demonstrations.

❖ Ask students if they know of (or have heard of) any lines from Shakespeare. What are they? (These may well turn out to be burlesqued versions of speeches from *Romeo and Juliet* or even *Richard III*.) Share these along with any humor attending them. Relate the responses to what you will be studying in the unit. After all, studying Shakespeare is fun — not something to dread.

❖ Remind students that Shakespeare's plays were on stage in London when the first English settlements in America were being established. (Jamestown was founded in 1607, and Shakespeare died in 1616.)

❖ Emphasize Shakespeare's popularity. Everyone — nobility and common folk alike—went to see his plays. Explain that he not only wrote scripts but also took an active part in the business end of play production and probably performed some parts on stage as well.

❖ Emphasize the power of plays today—TV drama, movies, videos—and relate that universal appeal to the tremendous popularity of comedy, tragedy, and history plays of the Elizabethan Age. The entertainment of that time was rich and varied, just as it is today.

About the Author

William Shakespeare was born into a reasonably well-to-do family. His father, John Shakespeare, was an established businessman in Stratford-upon-Avon who dealt in leather and glovemaking and who rose in town importance from being chamberlain and alderman to high bailiff, much like being a mayor today. William Shakespeare's mother, Mary Arden, came from a prominent Catholic family, although there is no evidence to support a conclusion that during those Elizabethan Protestant times Shakespeare himself was ever a secret Catholic.

William Shakespeare was almost certainly born in the house now known as The Birthplace. It was the custom to baptize a child three days after birth, and since church records at Holy Trinity Church in Stratford show his baptism to have been April 26, 1564, he is assumed to have been born April 23. The only records kept of births, marriages, and deaths were those kept by the church. He is believed to have attended school in the half-timbered building which still stands in Stratford, and some think he taught there for a short time, as well. He married Anne Hathaway when he was 18 and she was 26. They became the parents of three children—Susanna, and two years later, twins Judith and Hamnet.

No one knows for sure what Shakespeare did from 1585 to 1592, but by 1592 he was being mentioned as an "upstart crow" by a jealous rival dramatist in London. His first three plays were *Henry VI*, *Titus Andronicus*, and *The Comedy of Errors*. The theaters of London were closed between the years of 1592 to 1594 because of the bubonic plague, and during this time Shakespeare wrote his poem "Venus and Adonis" and began writing his sonnets.

In 1594 the plague was over, and Shakespeare helped form the Lord Chamberlain's Men, which became London's premier acting company in which he was both actor and playwright. Queen Elizabeth placed the company under her protection. This was very important because a religious group called the Puritans were trying to shut down the theaters for being sinful and attracting the wrong sorts of people. The queen loved the theater and the arts, so Shakespeare's company was able to enjoy 14 productive years until her death in 1603. At that time, King James I continued royal patronage, and thereafter the company was known as The King's Men.

Shakespeare's plays and poetry were very popular, and from the beginning of his writing until his death in 1616 he wrote 37 plays, 154 sonnets, and other poetry. Around 1610 he left London for good and retired to his home in Stratford where he became an important member of the local gentry. In 1613 he collaborated with John Fletcher on *Henry VIII*, *The Two Noble Kinsmen*, and a play which has since become lost, named *Cardenio*. He died in Stratford in April 1616.

Reading Response Journals

Much of the research into how good readers read and what the differences are between "good" and "bad" readers indicates that competent readers personalize their reading in ways that less competent readers do not. Competent readers put themselves into a story and relate personally to the characters in it. They visualize the story and its characters, and they respond to what they read with both their minds and their emotions. They live the story vicariously.

Helping your students to personally experience what they read in this way can improve their reading comprehension. Response journals are an excellent way to personalize the reading. Structuring student responses by giving specific questions to be answered can help your students focus more on the content of the reading, and open-ended questions may stimulate thinking about the emotional import of events to the characters. Sample questions are included with the lessons for each play.

Try some of these ideas with your students.

❖ Tell the students the purpose of the journal is to give them a format for recording their thoughts and feelings about what they read.

❖ Before the day's reading, provide the question to be answered to enable students to focus on that aspect of the reading and allow for more thoughtful responses.

❖ Provide any historical or cultural information the students need to help them place events into context and relate them to their own lives either by comparison or contrast. Emphasize the state of the world as Shakespeare and his contemporaries saw it.

❖ Use a wide variety of reading strategies and stop occasionally to discuss events or characters as the action of the play proceeds. Serve as a model by reading to students as they follow along. Because Shakespeare's plays are intended to be both oral and visual, include much oral reading and discussion about why the characters act as they do.

❖ Define literary terms such as *plot, allusion, motivation,* and *point of view,* and have students record them in their journals. The students will then have a ready guide to the terms when needed.

❖ To encourage students to make fullest use of journals, allow them to be used as open books during quizzes.

❖ If possible, keep the journals in the classroom. This will keep them neat, maintain their availability, and let students know that you consider them to be an important part of their study.

Shakespeare's World

The way in which Shakespeare and the people around him viewed the world was much different from the way it is viewed today. They saw the world like a huge morality play written, staged, and directed by God. *In As You Like It* Shakespeare wrote,

> *All the world's a stage,*
> *And all the men and women merely players.*
> *They have their exits and their entrances;*
> *And one man in his time plays many parts.*

In this play there was a contrast between good and evil, and events occurred in order to create a balance between the two. If the king or queen turned out to be cruel and tyrannical, or if a family was struck by a devastating illness or misfortune, it was because God was punishing them. Going against what was taught to be God's will would lead inevitably to severe punishment and ultimately to hell.

There was no mistaking right and wrong, for it was all based on the lessons taught by the Church. God was ruler of everything and everyone. The Church and its leaders were representatives of God on earth, and the king was king by divine right. Everyone else was at lower levels below the king and the Church (as in the pyramid below) with noblemen and churchmen above the common people. Children had no rights except those allowed them by their parents. Teenagers had to obey every wish of their parents until marriage, and marriage was usually arranged by the parents, especially in the upper classes. A wife was obliged to obey her husband. This diagram illustrates what the Elizabethans saw as their priorities on earth. How do you see yours? Complete the activity on page 10.

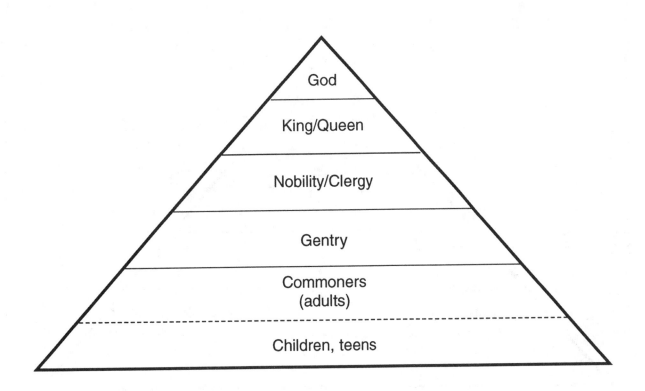

Setting Priorities

All people believe that certain things are more important in life than other things. Deciding those things is what we call setting priorities. Shakespeare and his fellow Elizabethans knew exactly what their priorities were. Everyone had his place in life and his duty to fulfill. One did not question those in power, such as parents, church, or king. One did exactly what one was supposed to do within one's station in life, or one was severely punished. This was what kept the world in balance.

What are your priorities? What do you see as being the most important things in your life? Beginning with number one below, list the things or people or goals in your life which you consider to be the most important and put them into your own pyramid of priorities. Then write a page or more explaining why these are so significant to you and why you have placed them in the order you have.

1. _____

2. _____

3. _____

4. _____

5. _____

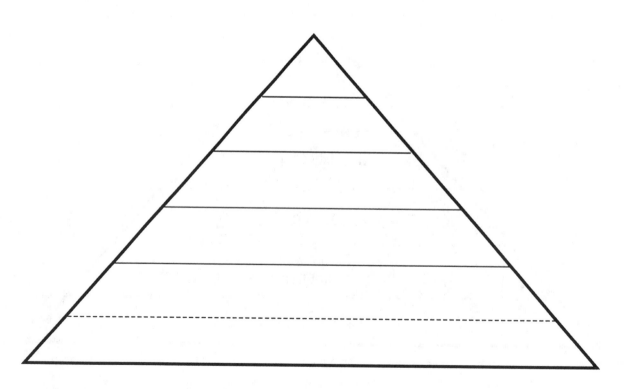

Priority Pyramid

Attending Shakespeare's Theater

Attending the theater in Shakespeare's time was very different from attending it now, and Shakespeare's own theater, the Globe, was unlike any modern one. It was probably round, or nearly so, and the roof covered only the outside galleries; thus, many who went to see the plays got wet in the frequent London rains. The stage jutted out into the audience, and the actors were surrounded on three sides by people who paid to see the performance.

Nearly half the theater-goers stood on the ground around the stage; they were called "groundlings," and they were a rowdy bunch, eating, talking and yelling out anything which took their fancy at the moment. People paying higher prices got seats in the galleries for their money and a roof to keep off the rain.

No one went to the theater at night. There were no electric stage lights, and the stage was in the middle of the audience, lighted by the sun. There was no scenery and very few props. There were no costumes except for any which the actors acquired for themselves, so there might be all manner of styles and periods of dress on the stage at one time.

Today no courteous theater-goer would think of walking around while a play was on, but Shakespeare's audiences, especially the groundlings, made no pretense of courtesy, and the playwright who, after all, had been an actor himself, knew he had better write a play filled with action and good stories or he would soon lose the attention of his audience. Shakespeare's plays are action-packed with all sorts of sword play and buffoonery.

In Shakespeare's time no women or girls acted in the plays, which is probably the main reason there are many more men's than women's parts in his plays. For a woman to act in a play would have been a shameless and serious breach of social custom. Women were played by men, and girls and young women were played by young men or boys who were carefully taught by the older actors. Only later in the seventeenth century did women and girls act, and even then an actress was considered somewhat daring and her character a little suspect.

In 1613 the old Globe Theatre burned to the ground after being set on fire by a spark from a cannon during a performance of *Henry VIII*.

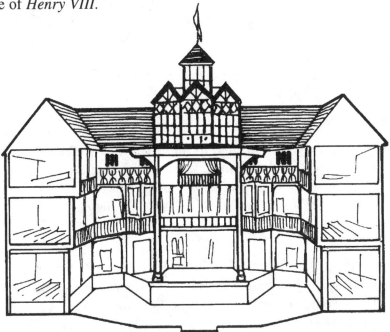

Scenery, Stage Properties, and Costumes

Today's audiences are accustomed to watching movies and television programs in which sets and costumes are realistic. If the story takes place in a park, we expect the background scenery to be of a park, and if the story takes place during the 1700s, we expect the sets, properties, and costumes to be from that time.

Shakespeare's plays were written for stages on which there were few, if any, sets or properties—props, as they are now called—so the actors had to tell the audience where the story took place. The members of the audience, for their part, had to listen to where the setting of the play was and use their imaginations. For example, just before *Richard III,* they would be told the setting was a street in London. In *Romeo and Juliet* the chorus, in a prologue, tells the audience the play is about two households in Verona. In *Much Ado About Nothing* Leonato says, "Don Pedro . . . comes this night to Messina." If he is coming to Messina, it is where the action of the play is going to take place.

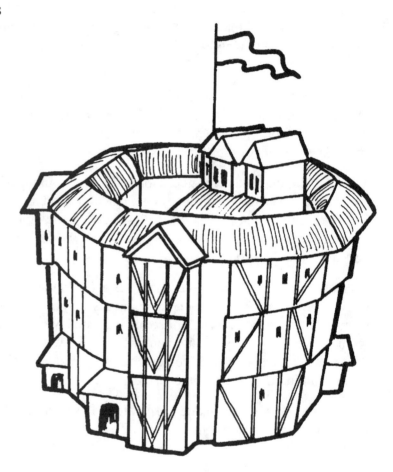

A list of properties for a play might be as simple as one golden fleece, one bay tree, three imperial crowns, a ghost's crown, a box to be used as a table or chair, and Neptune's fork and garland. Except for these, there might be no scenery at all. As far as costumes were concerned, they could be almost anything the actor wanted. If the play was about Romans such as *Julius Caesar* or *Titus Andronicus* and the actors wore armor, the armor they wore would probably have been sixteenth century armor rather than Roman armor.

This creates what is called an *anachronism,* an error in time, with the actors wearing costumes from one time period while the play is set in another. Shakespeare's audience did not mind this, however, because even though the plays were set in many different periods of time and many different places, the plays were really more about the England of his time than anything else.

Activity

Choose one of the three plays in this unit. In groups of four or five, list the properties you think would be absolutely necessary for the play to be successful. For example do you think you would have to have fencing swords or a balcony in *Romeo and Juliet* or a crown and throne in *Richard III?*

Men's Clothing

In Elizabethan times men's clothing was as colorful as that of the ladies, but men wanted to look manly, so they wore clothing in the shape of armor with broad shoulders, broad hips, and narrow waists. It could be compared to a suit of armor.

❖ *Doublet:* like a breastplate, covers back and chest, ridges down front; wings at shoulders

❖ *Sleeves*: separate garments, tight at wrists

❖ *Hose:* covered the body from waist down

❖ *Ruff:* stiffly starched ruffles at the neck, usually white

❖ *Hats:* of many different shapes, usually had a band, worn indoors

❖ *Cloaks:* capes

❖ *Gowns:* like cloaks but closed in front, fitted at the shoulders

The doublet was stuffed with horsehair, wool, or rags so it would keep its shape. The sleeves were tied to the doublet with laces. The upper parts of the hose were stuffed to make them stick out. Sometimes breeches, or *Venetians,* were worn over the hose. Cloaks, worn over the doublet, were very fashionable and made in different lengths but were usually short. Hats were worn indoors to keep warm.

Women's Clothing

Elizabethan women wanted their clothing to look much like that of the men, with broad shoulders, wide hips, and slim waists. Compare the drawing below to that of men's clothing on page 13 and notice how similar it was to that of the Elizabethan men except for the kirtle. Women's dresses were not made all in one piece as they usually are today. Instead, women wore two or more garments as one dress.

❖ *Bodice:* came down to the waist; above the neckline a separate garment called a "partlet" or jewelry bodice had "wings" at shoulders and came to a point at the narrow waist

❖ *Sleeves:* separate garments held to the bodice with laces; tight at wrists, but full otherwise; stuffed to keep shape; sometimes had ruffs at wrists to match ruff at neck

❖ *Kirtle:* skirt often of different material from the bodice; framework underneath was called a farthingale, made of wire or whalebone, causing kirtle to stand out from the body

❖ *Headwear:* hats and hoods very popular; sometimes came to a point over middle of the forehead, giving face a heart shape; styled very much like men's hats

❖ *Hair:* worn in many different styles, but always brushed back from the forehead

❖ *Outer garments:* cloaks and gowns were like the men's; often wore a *safeguard* or overskirt to protect the kirtle, especially when riding horseback

The items of clothing worn by the nobility were quite elaborate at times, with fancy plumes and jeweled or embroidered fabrics.

After reading about both the men's and women's clothing, think about the following questions.

❖ Do you think the clothing of commoners was similar?

❖ How might their clothing have been different from that of the nobility?

❖ Would you want to have to wear this type of clothing?

Reading Shakespeare Aloud

Actor Richard Burton once said he loved the sound of Shakespeare's words because they made "such a beautiful noise." When he said this, he was referring to the way in which Shakespeare's words seem to come alive musically when they are spoken aloud.

All Shakespeare's plays and poetry were written to be said aloud, and it is sometimes difficult for a newcomer to his works to get a sense of how truly rich and lovely they are without learning first how his words sound. The Elizabethans loved the spoken word. When they went to a play, they went to listen, much as you would listen to a play on the radio, and not just to see it. This is one reason Shakespeare's plays are full of puns and *double entendres*—words with two meanings, with one meaning often being improper or indelicate.

Learning to read Shakespeare aloud is not as difficult as it might seem with all its unfamiliar words. The reason they are unfamiliar to us is that they are no longer used much or at all. Some hints on how to read Shakespeare aloud might help.

1. If possible, watch a film version of a Shakespearean play first. Listen to what is said and how it is said. This will help you get a feel for the rhythm of the play. Rhythm is very important when reading Shakespeare. Some words should be said quickly, others slowly. Try to understand the meaning of what is being said, and let yourself into the flow of the rhythm. You will probably understand more than you first thought you would.

2. You will certainly want to learn the meanings of some of the words with which you are unfamiliar. With many you can figure out the general intent without having to spend so much time in the dictionary that you forget what has happened in the story. When you cannot figure them out, look in the footnotes or glossary for help.

3. When in doubt as to how to say a line, remember that the greatest stress of a line usually comes at the end of the sentence. An example of this is a line in *Romeo and Juliet* which may be misunderstood if it is spoken incorrectly.

    "Wherefore art thou Romeo?" is sometimes said with an accent on the word *where,* although the accent should be placed on the name *Romeo.* Accenting the first word of this sentence suggests that Juliet is asking where Romeo is, when in fact she is asking, "Why are you named Romeo? Why are you the son of my family's enemy?"

4. Pay close attention to punctuation. When a line ends with a period, stop. If it ends with a comma, pause but do not completely stop. If the line does not end with punctuation, continue reading without stopping or pausing. You will be amazed at how much better you understand what is said.

Reading Shakespeare Aloud *(cont.)*

5. When an "ed" at the end of a word has an accent mark over it, pronounce the "ed" as a separate syllable. This will not change the meaning of the word, but it will continue the rhythm of the passage.

6. One last word on the meaning of Shakespeare's words. The words which you have the most trouble with will probably be the ones which we use today but give meanings different from those they had in Elizabethan times. For example these words and the defintions as used in *Romeo and Juliet* follow:

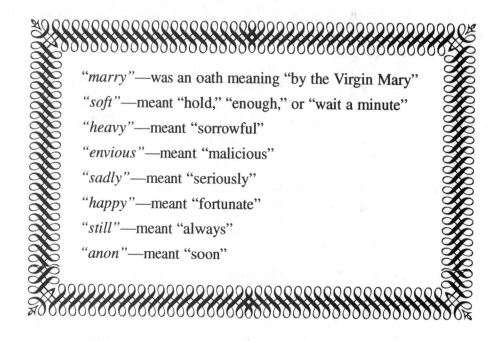

"*marry*"—was an oath meaning "by the Virgin Mary"

"*soft*"—meant "hold," "enough," or "wait a minute"

"*heavy*"—meant "sorrowful"

"*envious*"—meant "malicious"

"*sadly*"—meant "seriously"

"*happy*"—meant "fortunate"

"*still*"—meant "always"

"*anon*"—meant "soon"

Activities

Choose one of the following activities to do in appropriate-sized groups.

1. Do a Reader's Theater activity. In groups of three or four, choose a passage from *Romeo and Juliet, Much Ado About Nothing, Richard III,* or one of Shakespeare's sonnets to read aloud. Decide which person will do which part, practice reading the selection until you know it well, and perform it for the class.

2. In groups of three or four, one person takes the part of the "narrator" and reads a selection while the others act it out.

3. Choose a passage to render into modern English; then act it out.

Elizabethan Times

The following is a collection of common beliefs and practices in Shakespeare's England. Any one of these could be the start of a research project. It is important to remember when reading or seeing a Shakespeare play that the Bard himself in all probability also believed many of these things.

Beliefs About the Universe

Elizabethans believed the earth was the center of the universe and fixed firmly in place. All matter on earth was drawn to its center. Seven planets—the moon, Mercury, Venus, Sol (the sun), Mars, Jupiter, and Saturn—rotated around the earth, moving in concentric circles. The stars rotated in an eighth circle outside the planets. The planets in their motion around the earth made musical notes, and all of these sounds together formed a perfect harmony. Certain conjunctions of the planets were lucky, while others were unlucky. Planets gave out an ethereal fluid, or influence, which affected humans. Since the moon was the closest planet to earth, it affected the ebb and flow of tides and was very powerful. All the planets affected the affairs of earth. Because of these beliefs, astrologers thought they could predict future events by knowing the conjunction of stars, and the future course of a person's life could be known ahead of time by knowing the placement of the stars at that person's birth. This set of beliefs we call *astrology*.

The Almanac

Almanacs were small books which gave miscellaneous information. They were printed in two colors—black for the text and red for titles, special days, and other notable items. Church feast days and a calendar were included along with instructions for the best time for bleeding, purging, bathing, etc. An example would be "Draw the melancholike blood when the Moone is in Libra or Aquarius," referring to the then popular practice of drawing "bad" blood from a person as a medical treatment. An almanac also contained notes on convenient times for planting, the beginning and end of law terms, the dates when marriages could not be solemnized, dates of the eclipses of the sun and the moon, a vague prediction of what would happen during the year, a table showing how long the moon would shine each night, and a day-by-day forecast for the weather of the whole year. When astrologers and the makers of almanacs failed in their attempts to predict the future, they excused themselves by saying they could not foresee the will of God.

The Humors

Everything in the universe was thought to consist of four things: earth, air, fire, and water. Each of these elements was hostile to the others but could coexist when they were in the proper proportions. Since the human body was of this earth, it also consisted of these four elements, and medical practices and anatomy emphasized the need to understand how they worked together. Therefore, earth was identified as *black bile*, air was identified as *blood*, fire was *bile*, and water was *phlegm*.

Elizabethan Times *(cont.)*

Humors *(cont.)*

Each of the elements produced a certain temperament, which you could ascertain by looking at a person's complexion. Too much of the earth element produced a *melancholic* humor; too much air, a *sanguine* humor; too much fire a *choleric* humor; and too much water produced a *phlegmatic* humor. Good health meant that a person's humors were well-balanced against each other, but if one of them became too strong in relation to the others, the person became mentally and physically unbalanced. In Shakespeare's plays the word *humor* can be used to mean moisture, or any one of the four humors, but usually it means whim, obsession, temperament, mood, temper, or inclination. The melancholic humor was the humor talked about the most. Melancholic characters are often seen in the plays, and it was sometimes considered the mark of an intellectual. Hamlet was a man with a melancholic humor.

Bearbaiting and Bullbaiting

Two sports now considered inhumane were engaged in twice a week in London. In bearbaiting a bear was tied to a stake by a long rope. Four or five huge, fierce dogs called mastiffs were let into the pit with the bear, and they attacked the poor creature. When the dogs attacked, the bear fought back, although it was on a leash. Any dogs which survived the bear's retaliation were pulled off just before the bear was killed. In bullbaiting a bull was let into the pit and "worried" to death—teased and hurt until he died. Another "sport" was even worse than these. A pony was led into the pit with an ape fastened onto its back. Dogs were sent in after them, jumping and trying to get the ape while the terrified pony lashed out at the dogs. Other amusements included whipping a blind bear until blood was drawn.

Letters and Seals

When a legal document was drawn up between two people, the different copies were written by hand on a piece of parchment. The copies were then cut apart with a wavy or indented cut. This is where we get the word "indentures." The purpose was to prevent forgeries, and if there was a question whether one copy was genuine, it could be compared with the other copy. The copies were then folded and slits made through which a ribbon was passed. The impressing of a person's seal on the attached label completed the process. Today in the plays, letters are usually represented as having been rolled into a scroll, but they actually were written on a large sheet which was folded over with the writing inside. The writer's seal was impressed at the closure to ensure that the letter was not read in transit.

Elizabethan Times *(cont.)*

Heralds and Heraldry

Although heralds were more prominent during the Middle Ages than in Shakespeare's time, they still held an important place in the lives of the nobility. These men were concerned with the dignity and honor of the king, noblemen, and gentlemen. They organized all important ceremonies, particularly royal weddings, coronations, funerals, and certain ceremonial rites. They were official messengers of the king during war and peace, and they read royal proclamations to the general public. Their most important function, however, was to preserve the records of noble families and to grant coats of arms to men considered worthy to be called gentlemen. They were a kind of "social register" and "Who's Who" of their time.

Signs

In Shakespeare's England, houses were not numbered. Instead, each house displayed a sign which jutted out. Usually it was simple and may have been in the shape of a bell, dragon, or swan. Many homes in England are still named this way, and the public houses display signs which have been passed down for many years. Some signs contained recognizable symbols; for example, there were the red and white striped pole for a barber shop and the red lattice windows of a tavern.

Bowls

Bowls does not refer to a container (called *basins* in England) in which to mix up a cake. It refers to a favorite game in which a small "bowl," or ball (called a jack) was used as a mark at the end of a green lawn. The players roll their bowls toward the jack, and the one coming closest to it wins. When a bowl touches the jack, it was said to "kiss" it. Rather than being a perfect sphere, the bowl bulges somewhat to one side and is thus said to be biased, curving in an indirect course when it rolls.

The Great Household

In the large houses of the noblemen of Shakespeare's plays, it was fashionable to employ as many servants as possible. The nobleman's house was almost a small palace, and each department had its own set of servants. The head of these people, a man from a good family, was called the "gentleman servingman." Promising young scholars often took such a position. Likewise, a young lady from a good family might be employed to serve a family in this way, thereby learning polite behavior and how to run a household, serving until she married and had her own home. Such servants were not looked down upon and usually were equal in social status to the family for whom they worked.

Elizabethan Times *(cont.)*

Marriage Customs

Marriage, particularly for the good families and the wealthy, involved a rather complicated process. First there was the formal betrothal, which was a private affair. Then the banns were published. This meant that on three successive Sundays the minister publicly announced in church that the parties intended to be married and called on anyone having reason to think the couple should not be married to come and say why. If the couple wanted to hurry up the process, it was necessary to obtain a special license from the bishop. The wedding was usually an all-day occasion with a full ceremony and great celebration afterwards. Early on the morning of the wedding, the bridesmaids showed up at the bride's house. Shortly after that, the groom showed up at the bride's house with his attendants, musicians, and friends. The whole party then set out for the church, the bride in white with her hair down. After the ceremony, there was much feasting, dancing, drinking, and game-playing. After the bride and groom departed, the guests continued to celebrate.

Funeral Customs

For the noblemen, funeral services could be very elaborate with much pomp and circumstance. Enclosed in a covered coffin, the deceased was carried to the grave by pallbearers in black. Following the coffin was a long procession of mourners wearing hooded cloaks which completely covered them. The coat of arms of the deceased was painted on flags carried along in the procession, arranged and orchestrated by one of the family heralds, much as a holiday parade would now be conducted. After the funeral the mourners feasted, and money was given to the poor. The body was buried inside the church.

The funeral of Queen Elizabeth I on April 28, 1603, was by far the most elaborate of all. First the Knight Marshalls cleared the way, and then 240 poor women followed in groups of four. The servants, esquires, and knights came next, followed by the many servants from all of the royal household. Hundreds of additional mourners came in procession, including the queen's equerries, grooms, Privy Council members, chaplains, mayors, government officials, and then the chariot containing the queen's body in a lead coffin on which was a recumbent effigy, crowned and in Parliament robes. A canopy was carried over the coffin by four noblemen. The procession was completed by all the lords and ladies of the realm. Last of all were Sir Walter Raleigh, the Captain of the Guard, and all of the guard walking five-by-five and carrying their halberds turned downward. The streets of Westminster were filled with thousands of people sighing, groaning, and weeping as the procession passed and the queen was buried inside the church.

The Mail

There was no postal service for the general public, but there was a regular system of messengers on horseback used for official business. If an emergency existed, a postmaster at any of the stations along the route could conscript a horse belonging to anyone in order to get the message through. Messengers are frequently used in many of Shakespeare's plays.

Elizabethan Times *(cont.)*

Bells

Church bells rang for many occasions. They called the faithful to services on Sundays and holy days, announced good news, gave an alarm for fire or war and celebrated various occasions, including weddings and funerals. During fearful times such as an epidemic or the plague, the bells sounded constantly. When someone died, only a ominous single bell sounded.

Alchemy

Alchemists were the predecessors of today's chemists. Their work was based on the belief that all matter was composed of the four humors. Pure gold was thought to be a perfect metal in which all these qualities were perfectly combined, and the alchemist's primary quest was to find the "philosopher's stone" which could change other metals into gold. They also thought gold contained the "elixir of life" which could remedy the discord of the bodily humors and be a cure for all diseases. While the alchemists were basing their work on faulty premises, they did conduct original experiments and did not base their work entirely on tradition.

Dances

Elizabethans loved to dance, horrifying the Puritans, who thought dancing was of the devil. Some of the most popular dances included the *measure* (slow and solemn), the *pavan* (a dignified processional) the *galliard* (quick and lively), the *capriol* (one step was a jump into the air, clicking one's feet together), the *brawl*, and the *jig*.

Sports and Hunting

In addition to the gory spectator sports enjoyed by the Elizabethans, fencing was also a favorite. Betting often accompanied a fencing match, and one of the contestants would bet that he could hit his opponent a certain number of times. This happens in *Hamlet* when Laertes bets the king he will hit Hamlet 12 times before Hamlet can hit him nine times.

Hawking was very popular with gentlemen. Much time was spent on training a hawk or falcon and keeping it in good condition. The birds were captured wild and then tamed. The first step in training a hawk was to seal its eyes by passing a needle and thread through the lower eyelid of each eye, then tying the thread back over the bird's head. The eye could be opened at will by the falconer, but the temporary blinding made the bird easier to tame. A hood was placed over the bird's head and straps tied to his legs when he was taken outside. Then the hawk or falcon was ready to train to hunt other birds. Bells on the bird's legs allowed the falconer to keep track of it.

Activity

Choose one of these Elizabethan customs and write at least one page comparing and contrasting the Elizabethan custom with a related modern custom. You could, for example, compare Elizabethan sports with sports of today or Elizabethans' treatment of animals with today's. Bring your ideas to class and share them with your classmates.

Shakespeare Survey

Shakespeare began writing and acting in plays 400 years ago, and his plays are produced every day of every year. Some acting companies, such as the Royal Shakespeare Company of London and the Oregon Shakespeare Festival of Ashland, perform his plays annually for the pleasure of millions of people. More than 21,000 musical compositions have been inspired by Shakespeare's plays and poetry, with *Hamlet* alone accounting for 1,405.

Very few people in the English-speaking world have not heard of Shakespeare, but there may be many who have never seen a play by Shakespeare. In small groups or alone, survey your friends, teachers, family members, and neighbors, asking them the following questions:

	Yes	No
Have you ever heard of Shakespeare?		
Can you name at least one of his plays?		
Have you ever seen one of his plays?		
Have you ever seen a film made of one of his plays?		
Do you know the story of one of his plays?		

Record the answers you get in the chart provided, then come back together as a class and combine your tallies. Make a bar graph of the answers you get on a poster or large sheet of paper, and place on the class bulletin board.

	Yes	No
Has heard of Shakespeare		
Can name one of his plays		
Has seen one of his plays		
Has seen film of a play		
Knows story of a play		
Totals		

Quotation Survey

Quotations from Shakespeare fill almost 90 pages in Bartlett's *Familiar Quotations*. How many people can you find who have heard the following sayings or expressions? Place your tally marks in the blanks provided and combine your answers with those of your classmates' surveys.

Sayings	Have Heard	Have Not Heard
1. To be, or not to be, that is the question.		
2. A horse! A horse! My kingdom for a horse!		
3. All the world's a stage.		
4. What's in a name?		
5. Parting is such sweet sorrow.		
6. Household words		
7. What the dickens		
8. The primrose path		
9. Eaten me out of house and home		
10. Dead as a doornail		
11. An eyesore		
12. Foregone conclusion		
13. Bag and baggage		
14. A lean and hungry look		
15. Too much of a good thing		
16. The naked truth		
17. The game is up!		

History of the English Language

If you were transported by a time machine back to the England of five or six hundred years ago, you probably would not understand what people were saying to you because English was very different then. English is a growing language, and the history of the English language is long and complex. It began at least 8,000 years ago in the general area to the north of the Black Sea when a group of languages now called the Indo-European family of languages slowly emerged. In the history of English, two particular groups are important: the Romance (from Roman) languages, especially French and Latin, and the Germanic languages.

The forerunners of modern English came across the English Channel from continental Europe to the British Isles in about the fifth or sixth centuries A.D., brought by the Vikings and other invaders from Scandinavia, whom we now know as the Angles, Saxons, and Jutes. The languages they spoke were dialects of German which formed the basis of what we now call Old English. Both the grammar and the pronouns we use have their roots in the Germanic history of English.

In 1066 the Normans, a mixture of Scandinavian "Northmen" and French, invaded the islands and brought with them a whole new vocabulary which, in time, melded with the Old English to form the wonderfully rich language we now know. This was probably the single most important development in the entire history of English, for as much as one-fourth of our language has French origins. Most words ending with a silent *e*, or with *or, er, ent, ant, ion, ian,* or *ien* probably derive from French words. In fact, some methods of studying French are based on the fact that, even though the words are pronounced differently, many can be recognized by the English speaker because of the similarities in spelling. Such words are called *cognates.*

Other factors were also important in the growth of English. Many Latin and Greek words were added during the classical Renaissance of the 16th and 17th centuries. And when the English merchant seamen began to roam the world in the 15th and 16th centuries, they not only took with them their language (which was adopted by people in other lands) but they also brought back new words, so that English acquired words from Italian, Hindi, and Finnish, to name a just a few contributors to our present vocabulary.

English is still growing. Science and technology alone have added thousands of new words, and more are continually being invented.

Activity

1. Use a dictionary to find ten words which originally were French words. For example, after the definition for *report,* you will find [< Old French Report].

2. Invent a new word. Use any combination of words, such as Greek or Latin roots, to make a new word, as is often done in science and technology; or come up with a new use for a word commonly in existence, as is often done when slang words come into use.

Speaking with an English Tongue

English is sometimes called a living language because it is constantly in use by many people; and just as a living organism changes throughout life, so the English language is always changing. The English of Geoffrey Chaucer, who wrote *The Canterbury Tales* a little over a hundred years before Shakespeare wrote his plays, was quite different from what it is now, mainly because it was so much more full of Saxon, Germanic, and French words. (This stage of language development is usually called Middle English.) And as you can probably see, the language also changed during the hundred years between Chaucer and Shakespeare.

If you try reading aloud the following passage taken from the prologue to *The Canterbury Tales,* you will probably find that you understand much more than you think you will when you first look at it. As you read, write down what you think the passage says; that is, render it into your own words. Notice that each pair of lines rhymes. You do not have to make your version rhyme, although you may certainly try to rhyme it if you wish. When you have finished, look to the answer key and see how closely your version has come to that of someone else's.

Bifel that in that seson on a day,
In Southwerk at the Tabard as I lay,
Redy to wenden on my pilgrimage
To Caunterbury with ful devout corage,
At night was come into that hostelrye
Wel nyne and twenty in a companye
Of sondry folk, by aventure y-falle
In felaweshipe, and pilgrimes were they alle
That toward Caunterbury wolden ryde.
The chambres and the stables weren wyde,
And wel we weren esed atte beste.
And shortly, whan the sonne was to reste,
So hadde I spoken with hem everichon
That I was of hir felaweshipe anon,
And made forward erly for to ryse,
To take oure wey, ther as I yow devyse.
But natheles, whyl I have tyme and space,
Er that I ferther in this tale pace,
Me thinketh it acordaunt to resoun,
To telle yow al the condicioun
Of ech of hem, so as it semed me,
An whiche they were, and of what degree,
and eek in what array that they were inne:
And at a knight thanne wol I first biginne.

Student-Generated Vocabulary

Shakespeare's vocabulary was immense. Although his plays and poems contain many words no longer used, this is not a reason to hesitate introducing students to Shakespeare. Reading and listening to Shakespeare will allow your students the true pleasure that comes from a personal knowledge of literature considered by many to be the best ever written in English. An effective way to deal with Shakespearean vocabulary is to let the class generate the words. A way to accomplish this is given below.

Before reading each act, set a time limit for your students and give small groups of them one scene or one section of the act to go over together. The task of each group will be to read quickly through their section and list a given number of words to use for vocabulary study. Members of the group look up the words and record their meanings. When the class comes back together, the groups each share the words they discovered with the rest of the class and then write the words and definitions in the class dictionary.

A tablet of chart paper on an easel can constitute a very effective teaching aid when used for the class dictionary. The words can be written on it at the front of the classroom where each student can see it from his or her seat. Brightly colored markers can emphasize aspects of a word. In this way, during the reading of the act the words found difficult by the students are right in front of them, so they can quickly look up to see the word they don't know. Unlike the chalkboard with a limited amount of space which may become smudged over a period of days or weeks, chart paper contains a record of the words which may be returned to as needed.

Also, remind your students that one does not need to know the exact meaning of every word when reading Shakespeare. Many of the meanings become apparent in context. One does not need to know the meaning of the word "inductions" to understand what Richard is saying in the following lines:

> *Plots have I laid, inductions dangerous,*
> *By drunken prophecies, libels, and dreams,*
> *To set my brother Clarence and the King*
> *In deadly hate, the one against the other.*

Other ways to introduce new words can be found on page 27.

Vocabulary Activities

Since each of the plays will present the students with new or obscure words, using those words in a variety of ways will help the students retain their meanings.

In addition to the class dictionary, have students keep a personal vocabulary list of the words they encounter which they do not understand. Use these words in a variety of activities appropriate to the study of the plays to help them remember and understand the words. You might wish to try some of the suggestions below.

❖ **Illustrate a dictionary.**
The Elizabethan Age during which Shakespeare wrote and acted followed closely behind the first English printing press of William Caxton. Until this time most books had been laboriously printed by hand and were often lavishly illustrated. Artistic students might enjoy making illustrated dictionaries of their own, using bright colors and a lot of gold.

❖ **Compile a dictionary of slang terms.**
Shakespeare's plays were written for the common people as well as the nobility and are filled with slang terms of the time. What would a current dictionary of slang contain and how many of the words now used daily might be understood 50 years from now?

❖ **Compile a list of Dogberryisms.**
The constable Dogberry in *Much Ado About Nothing* continually confuses his listeners by using words incorrectly. Hunt out a number of these words, telling how he used them incorrectly and what word he intended instead.

❖ **Compile a glossary of words used in drama.**
Like any specialized area, dramatic works contain a number of words specific to that area. Sometimes words used specifically in one field are known as jargon. What would these words be for drama?

❖ **Illustrate obscure words.**
Shakespeare used some 29,000 words in his plays, many more than the average writer or speaker. Find some of the obscure words in any of the three plays and illustrate them for the way Shakespeare used them.

❖ **Take a survey.**
From the vocabulary list choose a number of words which you don't know. Write what you think the meaning of each word might be, and survey your family members, friends, and neighbors to see what they think the words mean. Bring the words back to class and compare the answers you got with those of your classmates. Then find the correct meanings. How close did you and the ones you surveyed come to figuring out the words on your own?

Etymology: Tracing a Word's Historical Roots

Did you know that you can trace the history of a word to learn what language it came from originally and what it originally meant? The study of the historical development of a word and its meaning is called *etymology*.

English is one of the world's most complex languages because so many other languages have combined to make it what it is today. English began in England over 2,000 years ago with people who lived there at that time. Then during the Roman Empire, England was invaded by the Romans, and many Latin words came into the language. When the Vikings later invaded England, they donated Scandinavian words, particularly pronouns. The ancestors of today's Germans, who were called Angles, Saxons, and Jutes, invaded England in the fifth century and contributed many Germanic words, as well as the structure by which we string words together, called *grammar*. And in 1066, the Normans invaded and contributed French words.

Each time England was invaded, the language changed and grew to what it is now. It has not stopped growing. Each day sees new words added to the hundreds of thousands of ones we call English. Some of these words have their origins in science, where old Greek words are often used as the roots for scientific terms. Today's technology has contributed many more words, and, believe it or not, even common slang has a part in the constant changing of English.

Complete one or more of the following activities to gain an appreciation for the dynamic language called English and share what you learn with your classmates.

Activities

1. The etymology of a word can be found in the dictionary. For example, the word *hide*, meaning the skin of an animal, is followed by [OE *hyd*], which tells you that the word came from the Old English.

   Sample Entry: **hide**, n, the skin of an animal, either raw or tanned. Animal hide is made into leather. [OE *hyd*]

   The word *repent* is followed by [OFr. *repentir*], telling you that this word came from the Old French.

   Sample Entry: **repent**, v, to feel sorry for wrongdoing, to regret and seek forgiveness. I repent my past behavior and intend to change. [OFr. *repentir*]

   Look up 20 words of your choice and record the origin of each. Can you see any kind of pattern in the words you find?

2. Compile a computer dictionary of words which come from our new technology. Computers have not been around very long, yet they have had a tremendous impact on our language. Using your school computer lab text or the owner's manual of a computer, list all the words you can find which are new ones stemming from this modern piece of equipment.

3. Make a list of mass media words which have come into the language since television and mass communication have become so prevalent.

Romeo and Juliet

Romeo and Juliet

Summary

Is there anyone who does not already know the story of *Romeo and Juliet*? Of all the plays, books, and poems written for the English-speaking world, few come close to equaling the emotional impact of *Romeo and Juliet*, and no other can serve as a standard for idealized love like the story of this star-crossed couple. Indeed, this play stands for everything that is romantic and tragic. A teenaged boy and girl meet at a ball, fall in love, marry, and die within five days, victims of their families' feud and their parents' lack of understanding. During those five short days, the passion flows, and some of William Shakespeare's loveliest poetry is spoken by the young lovers. No one ever forgets the play which pictures Shakespeare's view of star-crossed lovers.

Sample Lesson Plans

Lesson 1

- ❖ Discuss the Elizabethan Age historically (pages 17–21).
- ❖ Discuss how Elizabethans, including Shakespeare, saw the world (page 9).
- ❖ Set your priorities (pages 9–10).
- ❖ Make Elizabethan half-masques (page 128).

Lesson 2

- ❖ Learn about sonnets and how to write them (pages 131–134).
- ❖ Identify the parts of a sonnet (page 131).
- ❖ Discuss the use of poetry for dialogue.
- ❖ Learn about Shakespeare's theater (page 11).

Lesson 3

- ❖ Show film of *Romeo and Juliet*.
- ❖ Complete a plot plan of *Romeo and Juliet* (page 37).

Lesson 4

- ❖ Take a survey of how many people know about Shakespeare (page 22).
- ❖ Find out how many people have heard Shakespeare quotes (page 23).
- ❖ Discuss reading Shakespeare aloud (pages 15–16).
- ❖ Read Act I of *Romeo and Juliet*.
- ❖ Discuss family feuds and vendettas.

Sample Lesson Plans *(cont.)*

Lesson 5

❖ Read Act II of *Romeo and Juliet*.

❖ Discuss Elizabethan morality and necessity of marriage before consummation of love (page 32).

❖ Learn to improve the air with sachets (page 127).

Lesson 6

❖ Read Act III.

❖ Discuss arranged marriages and reasons for them.

Lesson 7

❖ Read Act IV.

❖ Discuss the desperation which would cause Juliet to pretend to comply with her father's will while planning to fake suicide.

❖ Read Act V.

Lesson 8

❖ Finish reading Act V.

❖ Discuss the roles of men and women in the play.

❖ Write a prose version of *Romeo and Juliet*, giving it a different ending.

❖ Discuss the fifteenth and sixteenth centuries and emphasize that although *Romeo and Juliet* is set in Italy, Shakespeare never intended it to be accurate historically or even to be Italian. It is Elizabethan in style and world-view.

Overview of Activities

Setting the Stage

1. *Romeo and Juliet* takes place in Verona, Italy, sometime during the years preceding the reign of Queen Elizabeth, but where and when the story supposedly happened is not terribly important because Shakespeare made no attempt to be historically accurate. The characters could have lived in England or France or anywhere else, but the fact remains that the play was written for English people of the late sixteenth century. The world view expressed by the characters and the chorus was that of sixteenth century England. Compare the Elizabethan world view to that of our own, so the students have an understanding of where the characters are "coming from" conceptually and emotionally.

2. Learn about sonnets and how to write them. Discuss the importance of poetry to the educated Elizabethan and the classical use of poetry in drama. Point out that while Romeo is a rather bland, not-too-interesting young man of 15 when we first meet him in Act I, after he meets Juliet he speaks in sonnets. Why is that? Why would the act of falling in love turn his speech from prose to poetry?

Overview of Activities *(cont.)*

Setting the Stage *(cont.)*

---

3. Show a film version of *Romeo and Juliet*. Shakespeare's plays were not written to be read like novels, but to be performed on stage and to be experienced by an audience. While there have been thousands of productions of the play and several films, most have shown the title roles played by mature adults. The version by Franco Zeffirelli is unique in that the actress playing the 13-year-old Juliet was only 15, and the actor playing the 15-year-old Romeo was only 17 when they made the film. There is tremendous electricity between the young stars as there would be between two young people in the throes of first love. The film is superb, and seeing it before reading the play can help young people to better understand what truly wonderful drama Shakespeare wrote. However, before showing this or any version, **preview the film and make sure it is appropriate for your class**.

Enjoying the Play

---

1. Make Elizabethan half-masques so students will be able to relate to the masqued ball (page 128). Romeo is wearing a half-masque in Act I when he meets Juliet.

2. Write sonnets or other poems. Some young people will be embarrassed to write love poems, so emphasize that these poems do not have to be love poems but can be about any thoughts, emotions, or situations.

3. Discuss the differences between the English language of Shakespeare's time and our own. Invent some new words.

4. Read Shakespeare's words aloud. The plays were not written to be read silently but exuberantly and orally. Since there were no artificial lights and few, if any, stage props, the actors would tell the audience where they were and what time of day it was, unlike contemporary plays which show setting by the lighting and costumes.

5. Discuss family feuds and vendettas. Ask students to think of disagreements between families which were so severe that no members of one would have anything to do with the other. Is this a thing of the past?

6. Discuss the Elizabethan ideas of morality and marriage. What are the differences between theirs and modern ones? Why would families be so careful to preserve the rights of parents to choose mates for their children and to do it when they were so young? Some youngsters were betrothed before the age of 12, and a girl not married by 20 was considered a spinster. Young women who did not marry by a certain age were often sent to a convent or nunnery.

7. Research the Shakespearean theater. How was it different from our own?

8. Try to find out when women began acting in England. (England was the only European country where women were not allowed to act.) Discuss what kinds of problems would be presented for the play producer by having to use boys and young men to play the roles of girls and women. (Several of Shakespeare's plays have girls who were pretending to be boys.)

Overview of Activities *(cont.)*

Enjoying the Play (cont.)

9. Listen to Elizabethan music and learn about the many musical productions which have been composed for Shakespeare's plays. Complete the Elizabethan instruments activity on page 152.

10. Write a prose version of *Romeo and Juliet*, giving it a different ending. Do you think the play would work with a different, "happy" ending? Would the two young lovers be such sympathetic characters if their love had not been so tragic?

11. Make a chart comparing life in *Romeo and Juliet*'s time with life today. Use the comparison chart on page 117 to show the differences between medical treatment, educational opportunities, religious freedom, clothing, and means of travel.

12. Make a plot plan of *Romeo and Juliet*.

Extending the Play

1. Show the film of *West Side Story*, starring Natalie Wood. (Preview before showing and determine the appropriateness for your class.) It was written by Leonard Bernstein using the story of *Romeo and Juliet*, but set in New York City's Spanish Harlem in the 1950's. Tell the students that Shakespeare's plays can often be set in various times and places, and very often the alternate settings work, because the stories are so universal that the setting is not as important as the characters and their plight. How successful do they think the story is when transplanted to Spanish Harlem? *West Side Story* played for a long time on Broadway and has been produced many times. Is this because the story is one all people can relate to? Would it work as well if it were put into some other setting, such as the Los Angeles of the 1990s or the London of World War II?

2. The morality plays of medieval times were the forerunners of Shakespearean theater. In groups of four or five, rewrite *Romeo and Juliet* as a morality play (page 99). What lesson will your play have?

3. Discuss the differences between the manner in which rich and poor people lived during Elizabethan times. Were the Montagues rich or poor? How can you tell? What about the Capulets? Would being rich or poor have made a difference in the play? Why? How might the play have been different?

4. Compile a dictionary of Elizabethan words taken from *Romeo and Juliet* or another play by Shakespeare. Make a chart showing words we still use but which now have different meanings and words which are no longer used.

5. Shakespeare used a total of over 29,000 words in his plays — 23,000 more than were used in the King James Version of the Bible. Some of these words were slang. Use a library dictionary to determine some of the slang words he used. Compile a dictionary of slang words used by you and your friends. Choose ones you think will still be in use 100 years from now and write a rationale for why you think these words will last.

Romeo and Juliet

Making a Diorama to Scale

Making a reproduction of a thing so that it is relative in size to that thing is called "reducing it to scale." If you wanted to make the figures and buildings in a diorama one-tenth the size they are in real life, you would divide the real dimensions by ten, such as in this example.

> The scale of your diorama is 1/10. Therefore, your man who is really 6 feet tall would be 6 feet (72 inches or 1.8 meters) divided by 10 = 7.2 inches (.18 m) to scale.

Try these on for size.

1. A house is 12 feet (4 meters) tall; scale is $^1/_{12}$.

   How tall is the house to scale? _____

2. A balcony is 15 feet (5 meters) off the ground; scale is $^1/_{10}$.

   How far from the ground of your diorama is the balcony?_____

3. Romeo is 5 feet 10 inches (1.8 meters) tall; scale is $^1/_7$.

   How tall is Romeo to scale? _____

4. Juliet's room is 21 feet (6.3 meters) wide; scale is $^1/_{12}$. (She lived in a palace!)

   How wide is Juliet's room to scale? _____

5. Juliet is 5 feet 2 inches (1.65 meters) tall; scale is $^1/_{10}$.

   How tall is Juliet to scale?_____

6. Your bedroom at home is _____ long; scale is $^1/_{12}$. (Measure your room.)

   How long is your room to scale?_____

7. Your father is_____ tall; scale is $^1/_{10}$. (Ask your father or other adult male.)

   How tall is your father to scale? _____

8. The classroom is_____wide; scale is $^1/_{15}$. (Measure the room.)

   How wide is the classroom to scale?_____

9. The classroom ceiling is _____ high; scale is $^1/_8$. (Measure floor to ceiling.)

   How high is the classroom ceiling to scale? _____

10. One side of a baseball diamond is 90 feet (30 meters); scale is $^1/_{15}$.

    How long is one side of a baseball diamond to scale? _____

Theater Trivia

In watching a play or working in the theater, there are special terms that are used. See how many of these you can correctly identify. Name the item, character, or idea which each description represents. You may use parents, teachers, librarians, or printed materials as resources.

1. Dishes, furniture, and telephone used by an actor _____

2. The place where the action of a play takes place _____

3. People who watch the play _____

4. Person who organizes action, tells actors where to sit, stand, walk, how to act a part, etc. _____

5. Place where the action of a film or video takes place _____

6. Play which tells of actual events which happened long ago _____

7. Words an actor says _____

8. Play in which a good man dies or meets a terrible end _____

9. Person who describes what is happening as it happens _____

10. Person who writes a play _____

11. Actor who plays the main male character in a play _____

12. Actress who plays young woman in a play _____

13. Location of Shakespeare's Globe Theater _____

14. Moves an actor makes _____

15. A funny or silly play _____

16. Copies of the play the actors use _____

17. Drapery which hides the stage _____

18. All of the actors and actresses in a play _____

19. Sides of a stage _____

20. Audience's way of showing appreciation of play _____

What's in a Name?

How many words do you think you can find in the name *Shakespeare*? Now is your chance to find out. Here are the rules.

1. All words must contain at least four letters.

2. Letters may be used only as many times as they appear in the name. For example, you may use up to three "e's," but only one "p."

3. Only one form of a word may be used. For example, you may use either "hear" or "hears," not both.

4. You may not use proper nouns or slang words.

5. The time limit is 30 minutes. You may continue on the back of the this page.

❖ Shakespeare ❖

_____   _____   _____

_____   _____   _____

_____   _____   _____

_____   _____   _____

_____   _____   _____

_____   _____   _____

_____   _____   _____

_____   _____   _____

_____   _____   _____

_____   _____   _____

_____   _____   _____

_____   _____   _____

_____   _____   _____

_____   _____   _____

_____   _____   _____

_____   _____   _____

Plotting a Story

A story contains certain elements: *setting, characters,* and *plot.*

The *setting* of a story is where and when it happens.

The *characters* in a story are the people or animals the story is about.

The *plot* of a story is what happens in the story. It is the unfolding of one event after another in a certain order until the conclusion is reached. In a good story the events occur in an order which grabs and holds the interest of the reader, so he wants to continue reading until he finds out what happens at the end. The order in which events occur is important if the story is to seem real to the reader, and one event must logically follow another. An author carefully plans the story so the character(s) moves forward in a series of closely-linked episodes until the character solves (or fails to solve) the problem, or gets (or fails to get) what he/she wants.

Students sometimes think that a story just happens, that the author is suddenly struck by inspiration as a magical tale flows out through his/her fingertips onto the paper. That may happen once in a blue moon, but most stories are the result of systematic work on the part of the writer. Helping students to see that an author writes with intention can help them better understand the significance of what happens in the story and help them better appreciate the craft of the writer.

Using story frames and plot plans (pages 38–39) enables students to break down a story into its parts so that it is a little more easily understood.

Using the main story line in *Romeo and Juliet*, have the students complete the following story frames and plot plan. They can then use what they have written as a basis for writing a summary of the play.

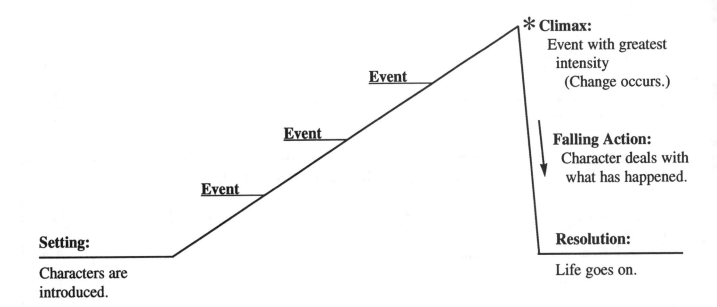

Sample Story Frames

Using the story frames, fill in the blanks with information from the play.

Setting Frame

This story takes place _____

_____.

I can tell because the author uses words like _____

_____

to tell where and when the story happens.

Plot Frame

This story begins when _____.

Then _____

and _____.

The story ends when _____

_____.

Character Comparison Frame

_____ and _____ are characters in the story.

_____ is _____, while

_____ is _____.

For one thing, _____ tries to _____ and

_____ learns a lesson when _____.

Plot Plan

Somebody _____

_____

_____

wanted _____

_____

_____

so _____

_____

_____

but _____

_____

_____

so _____

_____

_____

Finally _____

_____

_____

Negotiating Peace

The Capulet/Montague Lawsuit

Romeo and Juliet have both died because of misunderstanding and miscommunication between interested parties and because of the feud between their families. Now each family has filed a lawsuit against the other.

Because of your great negotiating skills, you have been named as the official negotiator whose responsibility is to bring the two families to a peace agreement with each other.

What advice do you give to each family? How does each family respond to the advice you give them?

Advice to the Capulets	**Response from the Capulets**

Advice to the Montagues	**Response from the Montagues**

40

Astrology or Astronomy: Which Is It?

Shakespeare and his contemporaries were very concerned with the stars. They believed that by knowing the way the stars were lined up at the time of birth, it was possible to tell the future. The mechanism they devised in order to do this was called a *horoscope*, and in Shakespeare's time a horoscope was considered a scientific tool. Some people still believe a horoscope can tell what lies ahead for you, but few people now consider it a scientific tool.

The true science of the stars and the heavens is called *astronomy*, and since the time of Shakespeare, it has helped us learn a great deal about the universe. We know the earth is not the center of the universe, as the Elizabethans thought, and that the sun is the center only of our own solar system. We know the moon is the only heavenly body that revolves around the earth and that there are other planets in our solar system which were unknown four centuries ago. We have sent men to walk on the moon, we have sent satellites orbiting around the earth, and we have sent spaceships millions and millions of miles away to send us information about far-off planets. We have begun unlocking the secrets of the universe, many of them through the science of astronomy.

Astrology is fun to think about sometimes, even though it is based on faulty ideas about the heavens. These are some of the basic beliefs of astrology:

❖ The stars, moon, and planets influence all earthly affairs. If one knows the meaning of their different placements at the time of one's birth, it is possible to foretell with a great deal of accuracy the future of that person, because each person's fate is determined by the stars.

❖ The movements of the heavenly bodies comprise the zodiac, which is a belt of the heavens encircling the earth and lying eight degrees on either side of the sun's yearly course. The zodiac is in the form of a circle which is divided into12 houses, or signs, each of which is 30 degrees. These signs and the dates within which they fall are as follows:

Aries (The Ram)—March 21 to April 19

Taurus (The Bull)—April 20 to May 20

Gemini (The Twins)—May 21 to June 20

Cancer (The Crab)—June 21 to July 22

Leo (The Lion)—July 23 to August 22

Virgo (The Virgin)—August 23 to September 22

Libra (The Scales)—September 23 to October 22

Scorpio (The Scorpion)—October 23 to November 21

Sagittarius (The Archer)—November 22 to December 21

Capricorn (The Goat)—December 22 to January 19

Aquarius (The Water Carrier)—January 20 to February 18

Pisces (The Fishes)—February 19 to March 20

Astrology or Astronomy: Which Is It? *(cont.)*

❖ During its yearly course, the sun passes into and out of each of these different signs, or belts. (Remember that in astrology the sun goes around the earth.)

❖ The sign under which a person is born will determine the kind of personality characteristics that person will have.

❖ Abnormal events in the heavens, such as an eclipse or the appearance of a comet, are omens of disaster.

Astrology is still a sort of popular pastime in that some people will consult an astrologer before undertaking any serious step in life. There are few newspapers which do not have a daily horoscope column, and most bookstores carry books and booklets about astrology. Often these books will have titles like *Star Signs for Lovers* or *The House of Stars*. Most people do not take these things seriously—but again, some do.

Activities

Use the list on the preceding page to learn what sign you were born under and complete one or more of the following activities:

1. Research your sign to see what kinds of personality traits you are said to have; then compare them with things you know about yourself. Do the traits listed for you on an astrological chart describe you? Or do they describe characteristics which almost any person would have?

2. Read your horoscope in the daily paper for a week. Did your daily horoscope correctly tell you what to expect for the day? Did you make any decisions based on it? What kinds of predictions did you read each day? Were they specific for you, or were they general ones which might have applied to anyone?

3. Draw your idea of what the zodiac with all its signs, such as the crab (Cancer) or the fishes (Pisces) would look like.

4. A) Draw up a full set of personality characteristics for two persons whom you know. (Be sure they are persons who have different characteristics.)

   B) Now find out their birthdays and check their characteristics (as you wrote them) against the characteristics listed in an astrological chart for those dates.

   C) Are there any similarities? List the similarities and differences.

   D) What conclusions, if any, can you draw from your activity?

42

Journal Questions

Use these questions for journals or for class discussions.

Act I

❖ How do we first learn of the feud between the Montagues and the Capulets?

❖ Why is Romeo unhappy when we first meet him in the play, and why does he change?

❖ Who does Capulet want to woo his daughter, and how does he intend to help him do it?

❖ Describe Juliet as she seems to you, and then as she seems to Romeo.

Act II

❖ What kind of person is Mercutio?

❖ Tell the story of Romeo and Juliet when he is standing under the balcony.

❖ What does Romeo ask Friar Lawrence to do for him, and how does the Friar respond?

❖ Describe the conspiracy among the two young lovers, Nurse, and Friar Lawrence. What is its result?

Act III

❖ What happens in the public place, and how does it affect Romeo and Juliet's plans?

❖ Why is Romeo shamed?

❖ Describe Juliet as Nurse describes her to Romeo.

❖ How does Lady Capulet misunderstand Juliet's sorrow?

❖ What does Juliet's father want her to do, and why can she not do it?

Act IV

❖ How does Friar Lawrence propose to help Juliet?

❖ What drastic measure does Juliet take to avoid marrying Paris?

❖ What does Nurse discover the following morning?

❖ How does Friar Lawrence deceive Juliet's parents?

❖ What does Capulet mean when he says, "Our solemn hymns to sullen dirges change?"

Act V

❖ What news does Balthasar give Romeo, and how does Romeo react?

❖ What is important about a purchase Romeo makes?

❖ Who visits Juliet's tomb, and what do he and Juliet together find?

❖ How does Juliet die?

❖ What does Friar Lawrence confess to the prince?

❖ Knowing what you now know about the way the Elizabethans saw the world, what is the moral of this play?

Responses

Explain the meanings of the following quotations from *Romeo and Juliet*.

1. "Down with the Capulets! Down with the Montagues!"

   _____

   _____

   _____

2. "Oh speak again, bright angel! For thou art
   As glorious to this night, being o'er my head
   As is a winged messenger of Heaven."

   _____

   _____

   _____

3. "Never was seen so black a day as this.
   Oh, woeful day, oh, woeful day!"

   _____

   _____

   _____

4. "Hold, there is forty ducats. Let me have a dram of poison."

   _____

   _____

   _____

5. "Take him and cut him out in little stars,
   And he will make the face of heaven so fine
   That all the world will be in love with night."

   _____

   _____

   _____

6. "Come, come with me, and we will make short work,
   For, by your leaves, you shall not stay alone
   Till Holy Church incorporate two in one."

   _____

   _____

   _____

Objective Test and Essay

Matching: Match the quotes with the characters who said them.

1. Tybalt   _____   A. "Why, lamb! Why, lady! Fie you slug-a-bed."

2. Lady Capulet   _____   B. "No warmth, no breath, shall testify thou livest."

3. Romeo   _____   C. "Take him and cut him out in little stars,…"

4. Montague   _____   D. "A plague on both your houses!"

5. Juliet   _____   E. "I will raise her statue in pure gold."

6. Nurse   _____   F. "Nurse, where's my daughter?"

7. Lady Montague   _____   G. "This, by his voice, should be a Montague."

8. Capulet   _____   H. "Dead art thou! Alack! my child is dead;…"

9. Mercutio   _____   I. "What light through yonder window breaks?"

10. Friar Lawrence   _____   J. "If love be rough with you, be rough with love.

True or False: Answer true or false in the blanks below.

1. _____   Romeo had never been in love before he loved Juliet.

2. _____   Friar Lawrence meddled in other people's business.

3. _____   Mercutio talked a lot about nothing.

4. _____   The Capulets and the Montagues had been friends for many years.

5. _____   Romeo first saw Juliet at a grand ball.

Short Answer: Write a brief response in the space provided.

1. Two people who secretly helped Romeo and Juliet to marry were _____

2. What happened in the streets of Verona? _____

3. Where was the famous love scene between the two young lovers? _____

4. Why did Romeo kill himself? _____

5. Name the man who married Romeo and Juliet. _____

Essay: Romeo and Juliet are often called "star-crossed lovers." Explain why this expression is used and tell how their story could have ended differently.

Much Ado About Nothing

46

Much Ado About Nothing

Summary

Much Ado About Nothing is one of Shakespeare's silliest romantic comedies, and it is also one of the most fun to watch. It has everyone from the sweetest, most innocent of girls in Hero, the wronged bride, to the most evil of villains, Don John, who does not even need a motive for wreaking destruction. It has Shakespeare's first great comic, Dogberry, who is so intent on impressing everyone with his intelligence that he ends up impressing them with his stupidity instead. But, above all else, the play has two of Shakespeare's most appealing lovers in Beatrice and Benedick.

Two separate plots wind their ways through *Much Ado About Nothing*. The main plot has Beatrice and Benedick cursing and insulting each other as though they were in a deep state of hate, when everyone around them can see they are thoroughly attracted to each other. Only after their friends trick them into doing so do the two admit reluctantly that they love each other.

In the minor plot the diabolical villain, Don John, out of pure spite and jealousy, falsely convinces Claudio that Hero is unfaithful. This takes place on the eve of his marriage. Stunned by the accusation, Hero pretends to be dead, and when the bumbling Dogberry and his merry watch stumble onto Don John's treachery, she magically returns to life, but only after the hasty Claudio has been made to suffer a deserved case of sorrow and remorse.

Of course, as must be true in a romantic comedy, all ends well and two weddings are proclaimed. There is no reason to look for reality in this play or in any other Shakespeare comedy, for that matter. It is taken for granted that as soon as you walk in the door of the theater you will suspend your sense of the real and succumb to the fun and inanity of it all. But that is what good theater is all about—to give you a chance to allow yourself to be manipulated for a couple of hours into thinking that the impossible can sometimes happen, and to give you the fun of watching it.

Sample Lesson Plans

Each of the lessons suggested below can take from one to several days to complete.

Lesson 1

- ❖ Introduce and complete some or all of the pre-reading activities found on pages 6–28.
- ❖ Read the play summary with your students (page 47).
- ❖ Generate the vocabulary list (ongoing during reading of the play).

Lesson 2

- ❖ Read Act I. As you read, place the vocabulary words in the context of the story and discuss their meanings.
- ❖ Do a vocabulary activity (page 27).
- ❖ Build a model pageant (page 126).
- ❖ Write and produce a morality play (page 99).
- ❖ Learn about Stratford-upon-Avon (page 50).

Sample Lesson Plans *(cont.)*

Lesson 3

- ❖ Read Act II. Place the vocabulary words in context and discuss their meanings.
- ❖ Do a vocabulary activity (page 27).
- ❖ Compile a slang dictionary (page 58).
- ❖ Write a story using Shakespeare quotes (page 101).

Lesson 4

- ❖ Read Act III. Place the vocabulary words in context and discuss their meanings.
- ❖ Learn about optical illusions (pages 54–55).
- ❖ Discuss the play in terms of history.

Lesson 5

- ❖ Read Act IV. Place the vocabulary words in context and discuss their meanings.
- ❖ Make a puppet theater (page 94).
- ❖ Write and produce a puppet play (page 92).
- ❖ Write a letter to Hero (page 53).

Lesson 6

- ❖ Read Act V. Place the vocabulary words in context and discuss their meanings.
- ❖ Make puppets (page 93).
- ❖ Learn about malapropisms (page 56).
- ❖ Learn how to convert Celsius temperatures to Fahrenheit (page 107).
- ❖ Find words in Shakespeare's name (page 36).

Lesson 7

- ❖ Discuss any questions your students may have about the play (page 61).
- ❖ Assign book report and research projects (page 148).
- ❖ Begin work on the culminating activities (page 149).

Lesson 8

- ❖ Discuss the student's options and enjoyment of the play.
- ❖ Provide a list of related reading for the students (page 169–171).

Lesson 9

- ❖ Celebrate the culminating activity, Festival of the Dramatic Arts and Cream Tea (page 160).

Overview of Activities

Setting the Stage

1. Several plots work together to form this play, the main story of which involves Claudio and Hero. Claudio is told that Hero, with whom he is in love, has been seen talking at her bedroom window with another lover, so he repudiates her publicly, an action that results in near tragedy but ends up happily. In the meantime, Benedick and Beatrice are tricked into acknowledging they are in love with each other, and the Keystone-Kops (slapstick) antics of the constable, Dogberry, lead to the downfall of arch-villain Don John. Don John says very little but hovers over the rest of the action because what he does say almost leads to disaster. Dogberry causes much consternation for everyone around him as he tries to solve a mystery. Despite there being little real sense to this play, it is one of Shakespeare's most amusing to watch. Do not look for logic or good sense in this one. Just enjoy it!

2. Learn the difference between comedy and tragedy. Discuss the fact that very little sometimes separates the two except a very thin line and that what is funny when it ends one way can be tragic when it ends another way.

Enjoying the Play

1. Learn about morality plays and build a model pageant. Discuss how Elizabethans were preoccupied with heaven and hell and all the ideas about judgment which existed for people whose lives revolved around the Church. Discuss what a tragedy it would have been for a girl who had never been with a man to be repudiated publicly as a person who had had affairs with men instead of remaining chaste until marriage.

2. Learn about slang. Discuss the fact that most languages have some form of slang. Discuss some of the slang used by the students now and how it is different from the slang their parents used as teenagers.

3. Help students come to a realization of the effects Shakespeare's works have had on the English language. How many expressions original with Shakespeare do they know? Can they find expressions of Shakespeare's which are not in the three plays in this book but which they have heard in use?

4. Use the activity on optical illusions to begin a discussion about how things are not always the way they seem to be on the surface. What other kinds of illusions can they think of?

5. Learn about malapropisms and Dogberryisms. Discuss how words can be used to confuse or to deceive.

Extending the Play

1. Rewrite *Much Ado About Nothing* as a puppet play.

2. Assign literature reports and research projects based on concepts or ideas which the students have encountered with this play.

3. Show the Kenneth Branagh film of *Much Ado About Nothing*. (Preview before showing and determine the appropriateness for your class.) How does the film differ from the ways in which the students had conceived the play? How would the play have been different with boys playing the parts of the female characters?

Shakespeare's Home: Stratford-upon-Avon

Stratford-upon-Avon is a beautiful little town in a lovely area of England known as the Cotswolds. People go there from all over the world all year long to visit the birthplace of Shakespeare. Begun in the Middle Ages as a market town, it was the place where farmers brought their produce to sell. The country people would raise all the food they needed for their families, sell the rest, and in that way be able to buy a few of the items for which they needed money.

A man named Hugh Clopton was important in Stratford's growth. He was a mercer, a dealer in textiles, who became very wealthy. In 1483 he built a large brick house on Chapel Street. What was unusual about this house was that although the Romans had made and used bricks while they were in England, the art of brickmaking had been forgotten for a thousand years until Clopton built New Place. This is the same house which Shakespeare bought and lived in the last years of his life. The house was timber-framed like the other houses nearby, but instead of wattle-and-daub panels to fill the gaps between the timber, Clopton used bricks.

Clopton built many things in Stratford besides his house. He started with the Guild Chapel, almost opposite from New Place, giving it a steeple and stained glass windows. The interior walls he covered with beautiful paintings.

The most striking achievement of Clopton's in Stratford was the magnificent stone bridge he had built over the river Avon. He had workmen drive closely-packed piles in circles; then the men cleared away the mud and sand from inside the wooden rings and dug down to make holes for the bridge's foundations. When they finished, the bridge with its 14 arches was much as we see it now. Of course, it is called the Clopton Bridge.

Visitors may visit the Shakespeare birthplace, the Guild Chapel, Trinity Church, where Shakespeare is buried, the homes of his daughter and granddaughter, and the school he attended and at which he may have taught before going to London. New Place, where Shakespeare died, no longer stands. In 1753, Reverend Francis Gastrell, who then owned the house, displayed a most irreverent disposition by having a temper fit about the many pilgrims who came to stare at the house and play homage. In spite, he had the building, which would have been second in interest only to the birthhplace, demolished forever. The garden remains, though, along with a mulberry tree said to have been planted by Shakespeare.

English Cottages of Shakespeare's Time

The timber-framed, thatch-roofed cottages of England are recognized around the world as being "typically English." Many of these picturesque houses were built during the Elizabethan period when Shakespeare wrote his plays, and people still live in them today. The cottage known as Anne Hathaway's Cottage, because it was the family home of Shakespeare's wife, is one such house.

The houses are said to be "timber-framed," because whole young trees were cut and "chopped square" to use as the support structures for the houses. Thatched roofs were made by taking a hefty amount of straw and tying it down in such as way that it made a weather-tight covering for the house. The houses were built of timber and straw in areas which were some distance from stone quarries or in places where the right kind of clay to make bricks did not exist. At that time, the transport of such heavy building materials was not possible for the average person, so people built their homes of whatever was available to them. Straw and timber are quite flammable, and it is remarkable that so many of these houses still stand to shelter the families who live in them.

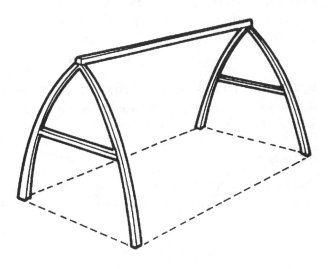

The simplest of the timber-framed houses was the *cruck house*. A cruck was the end frame in which the tree was split down the middle and the two pieces brought together at the top. A ridge piece went from one cruck to another, and a tie beam spread the two parts of the cruck as shown. The floor within the two crucks would be roughly a square.

A small cruck house might have only two crucks in its frame, while a larger house could be built by adding more crucks. A house could be enlarged by lengthening it. In fact, it could be made as long as one wished it to be. Other changes were more difficult, however. It could not easily be made wider or higher.

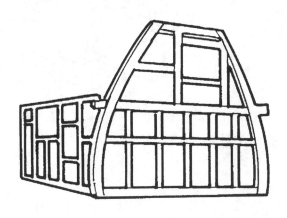

English Cottages of Shakespeare's Time *(cont.)*

After the framing was completed, it was filled in with a mixture called *wattle-and-daub* in which mud was spread over a mesh of twigs and sticks. The twigs and sticks helped to support the mud and give it strength when it had dried. This sounds as though the wall thus formed would not be very strong, but many houses built this way have stood through the centuries. Plaster was spread inside and outside over the wattle-and-daub between the timbers, and it was painted or whitewashed. If the timbers were of oak, they usually were not treated with any preservative, although in later years people often tarred them.

We see the contrast of the blackened timbers with the white stucco or plaster as a very attractive finish. However, during the sixteenth century plaster covered timbers as well as the wattle-and-daub. The covering of the timbers with plaster made them more watertight. It was only later that people chipped the plaster off the timbers to expose them. It is usually necessary to cover thatched roofs with a meshed wire such as chicken wire. This prevents rats and birds from burrowing into the straw to make their nests. Many of these roofs are made more picturesque by cutting the straw near the ridge of the roof into fanciful designs.

Until the sixteenth century most fireplaces were in the center of the floor with a hole in the roof for smoke to escape. As houses became larger and people had more choices as to how to build them, they began building fireplaces and chimneys as we now know them. When they began doing this, it became possible to add second stories to the houses.

By the latter part of the sixteenth century, bricks were becoming more available, and after that wattle-and-daub was no longer used for the walls. Most English houses are now made of brick or stone, and their roofs are either stone or tile.

Activity

Build a model cruck house. What will you use for framing? Will you fill your walls with wattle-and-daub? How will you finish your house? What roofing material will you use?

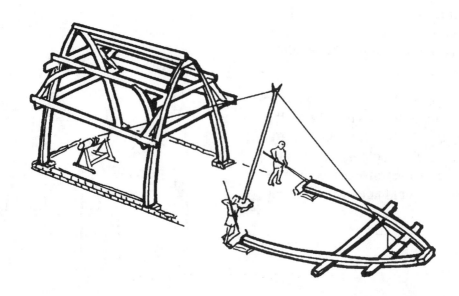

Write a Letter to Hero

Imagine that you were a guest at what you thought was going to be the wedding of Hero, who is a friend yours. Because you have known her all your life, you are sure that she is innocent of the charges which Claudio has leveled against her. What on earth can you say to her? In the space provided below, write her a letter to console her and try to make her feel better.

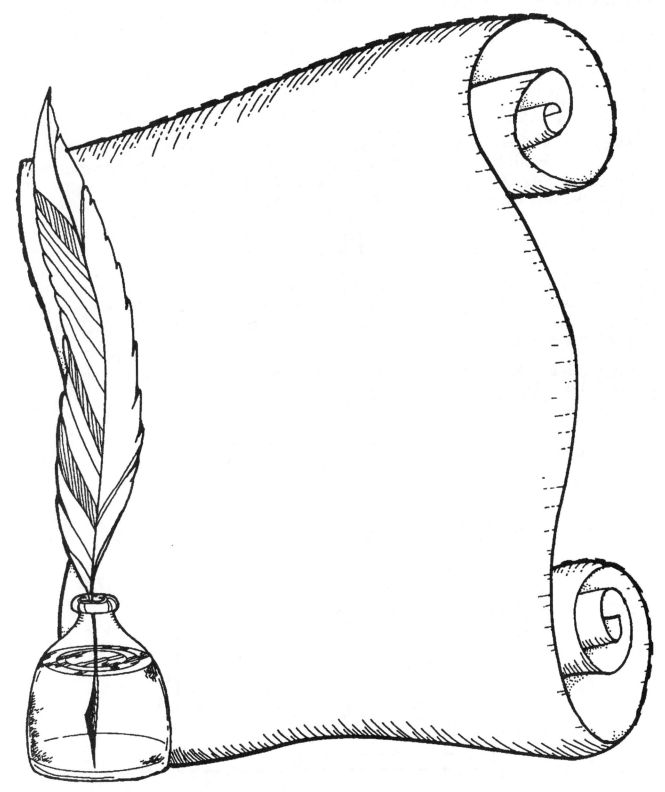

Optical Illusions

Look at these two lines. Which one do you think is longer, A or B?

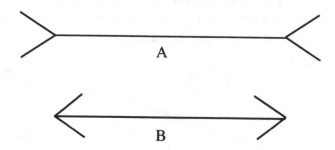

Ignoring the shorter lines projecting from the ends of lines A and B, measure A and B. The lines are exactly the same length, but they appear to be different lengths because the divergent lines projecting from line A fool the eyes into thinking line A is longer than line B. At the same time, the convergent lines projecting from the ends of line B fool the eyes into thinking line B is shorter than line A.

In *Much Ado About Nothing*, Claudio thinks he sees something which he does not see, and he makes a bad choice because of it. Many times our eyes fool us into thinking we see something we do not see, or we perceive something as different than it actually is. Eye witnesses to crimes often are incorrect in their judgments about what they have witnessed because each witness observes from a different angle, each seeing something a little different from what the other sees. We also sometimes tend to see what we expect to see, instead of what is. This is what happened to Claudio. He expected to see a certain thing, and, sure enough, he did.

Look at the picture below. What do you see? The profile of a lady? Or a side view of an urn? Both views would be correct. Go on to the next page.

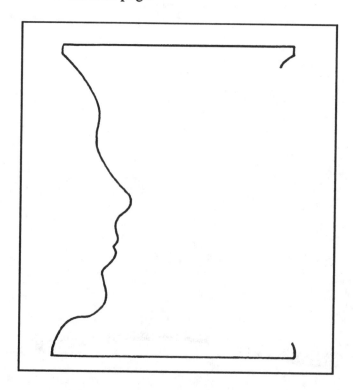

Optical Illusions *(cont.)*

Hold this paper about one foot (30 centimeters) from your eyes and stare hard at the ghost for 30 seconds. Then look immediately at the archway for ten seconds, and the ghost will appear there!

Look at these pictures carefully. Are the men in figure A the same size? Is the circle in figure B round? See how effective you can be in researching and then writing an explanation for each of these phenomena.

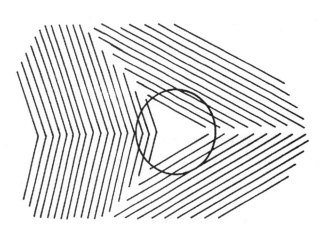

Dogberry and Malapropisms

Shakespeare must have had a lot of fun creating the character of Dogberry because he is one of Shakespeare's truly comic characters. Dogberry is rather like an Elizabethan Keystone Kop, the constable on duty who through bumbling and fumbling exposes Don John, the villain. From his mouth comes a constant stream of words we would call *malapropisms*—that is, words which are misused in a humorous way.

Malaprops

Some malapropisms substitute the wrong word for one or two words in a sentence so that the sentence provokes humor. Some examples of malapropisms follow:

- ❖ They lived in the Sarah Desert and traveled by Camelot.

- ❖ Certain areas of the desert are cultivated by irritation.

- ❖ David was a Hebrew king skilled at playing the liar.

- ❖ A myth is a female moth.

- ❖ Homer wrote *The Iliad* and the *Oddity*.

- ❖ We found it hard to understand his Scottish derelict.

- ❖ The doctor said to take milk of amnesia.

Dogberries

Have you ever known anyone who tries to use big words but ends up not making sense? That is what Dogberry does. Dogberry continually and in almost every sentence says at least one word which means the opposite of what he intends to say.

Some examples follow:

- ❖ "You are thought to be the most senseless and fit man."

- ❖ "Comparisons are odorous."

- ❖ "Thou shalt be condemned into everlasting redemption for this."

- ❖ "Dost thou not suspect my place?"

- ❖ "Come, bring away the plaintiffs."

What does each of these sentences mean? What do you think Dogberry intended to say instead?

Activity

In groups of three or four, write a short story using malapropisms. You will probably find it easiest to write the story first, then substitute the malapropisms. Remember to substitute words which sound very much like the original word. Afterwards, share your story with the rest of the class.

Buying Fabric for Costumes

Shakespeare's plays need little in the way of furnished sets, but the costumes for the plays can be quite elaborate and require much fabric and other materials. Remember, women's dresses were quite fancy, full-length, and often ornamented with all sorts of laces and beads. Calculate the materials needed in the following costumes.

1. If one woman's costume takes 9 yards (meters) of material, how many yards (meters) would be required to make one costume each for 8 women? _____

2. If Beatrice needs five costumes requiring 8, 10, 8, 11, and 12 yards (meters), and Hero needs six costumes requiring 9, 9, 11, 12, 10, and 13 yards (meters), what is the average number of yards (meters) of material needed for all the costumes? _____

    _____

3. One of Beatrice's costumes requires the following: 9 yards (meters) of fabric at $11.50 per yard (meter); four spools of thread at $4.99 each; and 17 yards (meters) of lace at $3.00 per yard (meter).

    How much will the materials for the costume cost? _____

4. If the costume maker of the above costume earns $15.50 per hour, and the costume takes 13 hours to make, what will be the total cost of the costume? _____

5. Don Pedro is a prince and as a prince, he must be very well dressed. His costume at the beginning of the play requires the following: 7 yards (meters) of velvet at $13.99 per yard (meter); leggings at $12.95 per pair; one pair of boots at $79.99 per pair, and a hat to match the velvet cape at $17.50.

    How much will his costume cost? _____

6. The costume maker who earns $15.50 per hour worked only four days per week but for nine hours each day. How much did he earn in one week? _____ One year? _____

7. The costumes last an average of six weeks for a leading actor or actress. If Beatrice needs five costumes and the play runs 54 weeks, how many costumes will she need to last the run of the play? _____

8. The wedding gown in *A Midsummer Night's Dream* has a very long train. The gown, including train and dress, takes 37 yards (meters) at $13.49 per yard per (meter), and the costume maker must spend 42 hours working on it at $15.50 per hour.

    How much will the wedding costume cost? _____

9. Ten soldier costumes cost $54.95 each to make plus $45.00 per pair for ten pairs of boots. How much do all the costumes and boots cost? _____

10. Sixteen of the characters in one play must wear wigs costing an average of $36.95 each.

    How much will all the wigs cost? _____

Update Your Dictionary

William Shakespeare used over 29,000 different words in his plays and poetry! That is 23,000 more than were used in the King James Version of the Bible, which was translated during the reign of King James I, Shakespeare's patron after the death of Queen Elizabeth I.

Shakespeare used a great many slang words of his time, and many of the words which cause us confusion do so because slang words tend to be superseded by new slang words after a relatively short time. Some of his puns, or word plays, are hard for us to understand because the words either mean something different now or are not even used in our modern English.

When Shakespeare wrote *Much Ado About Nothing*, there were no dictionaries. In fact, English had been considered worthy of being put into print for only the relatively short time of about a century. It would have made reading his plays much easier if there had been dictionaries, wouldn't it? But even today some dictionaries do not include slang words because of their short lives.

What are the meanings of these slang expressions?

couch potato _____

boob tube_____

colorize _____

totally awesome _____

rad _____

cool _____

chill out _____

Activity: In groups of four or five, compile a slang dictionary. Include as many slang expressions as you, your friends, your family members, the media, and your teachers use, as well as those used on television. Put all your entries into a class dictionary which you can display at the end of this unit. Illustrate as many as you can to make your definitions even more descriptive.

Shakespeare and Music

More of Shakespeare's plays and poems have been the inspiration for the music of major composers, both classical and modern, than have the writings of any other author. *A Shakespeare Music Catalogue* lists more than 21,000 musical compositions inspired by his works, 1,405 of them inspired by *Hamlet* alone.

Many of the compositions are operas which were based on the plays. Shakespeare was 33 when the first opera was written. Although he probably never heard one, the plots of many of his plays, particularly the tragedies, are very suitable for adaptation to that musical genre. Twenty-three of his 37 plays have been made into operas, many of them more than once. One of the best is probably Verdi's *Otello*, with its growling trumpets, screaming flutes, and pounding tympani. Verdi also wrote his *Falstaff* based on Shakespeare's *The Merry Wives of Windsor*.

Prokofiev's ballet of *Romeo and Juliet* is one of the most beautiful pieces of musical theater ever composed, and the meeting of the two lovers at a masked ball is awesome. Mendelssohn's *A Midsummer Night's Dream* is quite magical; after all, is there anyone who has never heard its "Wedding March" to which millions of newly-married couples have walked down the aisle?

Several modern musical comedies have been based on Shakespeare plays. *The Boys from Syracuse* is a musical takeoff on *The Comedy of Errors*. *Kiss Me Kate* is based on *The Taming of the Shrew,* and *West Side Story,* the heartbreaking story of star-crossed lovers in New York's Spanish Harlem, was based on *Romeo and Juliet*.

Shakespeare himself wrote many song lyrics within his plays. Some of these songs were sung by the prepubescent boys who played girls and women on the English stage when females were not allowed to perform. Many of the songs are rather like interludes which distill the atmosphere of a play. "Under the Greenwood Tree," from *As You Like It,* "When Daffodils Begin to Peer," from *The Winter's Tale,* and "For the Rain It Raineth Everyday," from *Twelfth Night,* are three such songs. Can you find the song in *Much Ado About Nothing*?

Activity

Do some research to find a recording of a piece of music which was inspired by Shakespeare or which has come down from Elizabethan times. Your school librarian or the public librarian should be able to help you, and the bibliography on page 170 lists some cassette tapes of Elizabethan music which may be ordered. Once you have the music, play it for your class. As a group compare it to some contemporary music. Does it sound alike or different? Do you think it might be popular today? Give your reasons.

Family and Marriage Counseling

Benedick and Beatrice were married. Unfortunately, just as it is said that a leopard cannot change his spots, so too, the pair of them have a great deal of difficulty in getting along with each other after having spent so much time doing just the opposite.

The situation is complicated by the fact that now they have a child they both love very much.

You have been engaged as a family and marriage counselor to try to help them sort out their problems and deal with the things which cause them to bicker and insult each other, even though they still love each other dearly.

How will you do this?

Write the advice you will give to each of them. How will your advice for Beatrice be different from that for Benedick?

Advice to Benedick

Advice to Beatrice

Journal Questions

Use these questions for journals or for class discussions.

Act I

❖ What is Beatrice's opinion of Benedick? What is Benedick's opinion of Beatrice?

❖ What does Claudio confess to Benedick and Don Pedro, and what does he ask Don Pedro to do about it?

❖ How does Don John see himself?

❖ What does Don John intend to do to Claudio's plans?

Act II

❖ Does Beatrice see through Don John? Explain your answer.

❖ How does Beatrice disappoint Don Pedro?

❖ Why is Beatrice not married?

❖ Who helps Don John accomplish his plan, and how?

Act III

❖ How do Hero, Margaret, and Ursula conspire together?

❖ What does Beatrice hear that sets her mind questioning?

❖ Where does Don John take Claudio, and what do they see?

❖ What can you make of what Dogberry says? Does he speak plain English?

❖ Why does the watch put Conrade and Borachio in jail?

Act IV

❖ How does Claudio answer the Friar on his wedding day?

❖ What does Beatrice mean when she says, "Oh, on my soul, my cousin is belied"?

❖ Who does Benedick love, and how can you tell?

❖ Describe Dogberry's manner of speaking.

Act V

❖ What does Leonato tell Claudio about his daughter?

❖ How does Claudio learn the truth about Hero?

❖ How does Leonato propose that Claudio still make up for the wrong he did Hero?

❖ What is the meaning of these words?

> "The god of love,
> That sits above,
> And knows me, and knows me,
> How pitiful I deserve—"

❖ What does Claudio say he will do yearly?

Responses

Explain the meanings of each of these quotations in *Much Ado About Nothing*.

1. "I wonder that you will still be talking, Signior Benedick. Nobody marks you."

    _____

2. "What, my dear Lady Disdain! Are you yet living?"

    _____

3. "…I am returned and…war thoughts
    Have left their places vacant, in their rooms
    Come thronging soft and delicate desires,
    All prompting me how fair young Hero is,
    Saying I liked her ere I went to wars."

    _____

4. "If I can cross him anyway, I bless myself every way."

    _____

5. "How tartly that gentleman looks. I never can see him, but I am heartburned an hour after."

    _____

6. "I have wooed in thy name, and fair Hero is won."

    _____

7. "Hey nonny, nonny."

    _____

8. "My talk to thee must be how Benedick
    Is sick in love with Beatrice."

    _____

9. "I came hither to tell you, for she has been too long a-talking of, the lady is disloyal."

    _____

10. "Our watch, sir, have indeed comprehended two aspicious persons, and we would have them this
    morning examined before your worship."

    _____

11. "There, Leonato, take her back again.
    Give not this rotten orange to your friend."

    _____

12. "Thou has wronged mine innocent child…
    And she lies buried with her ancestors."

    _____

13. "Suffer love—a good epithet! I do suffer love indeed, for I love thee against my will."

    _____

14. "Another Hero!"

    _____

15. "Peace! I will stop your mouth."

    _____

Objective Test and Essay

Matching: Match the descriptions of the characters with their names.

1. Hero   _____   A. Follower of Don John

2. Friar Francis   _____   B. States Benedick is the last man she'd love

3. Don John   _____   C. Father of Hero

4. Claudio   _____   D. Faints at her wedding

5. Benedick   _____   E. Has faith in a bride's virtue

6. Margaret   _____   F. Has his wedding proposal turned down

7. Beatrice   _____   G. Is used by Borachio to trick Claudio

8. Dogberry   _____   H. Falls for a dirty trick

9. Conrade   _____   I. Leonato's brother

10. Don Pedro   _____   J. Says the opposite of what he means

11. Leonato   _____   K. Is jealous of Claudio

12. Antonio   _____   L. Talks too much for Beatrice

True or False: Answer true or false in the blanks below.

1. _____   Everyone knows Beatrice and Benedick love each other except themselves.

2. _____   Don John wants only the best for his niece.

3. _____   Dogberry and the watch set out to trap the villains.

4. _____   When told his daughter is unfaithful, Leonato immediately disowns her.

5. _____   Hero does what Don John said she did.

Short Answer: Write a brief response to each question in the space provided.

1. Who lies about the bride? _____

2. Name three complaints that Beatrice has about Benedick. _____

3. What does Margaret do that is so wrong? _____

4. Where does *Much Ado About Nothing* take place? _____

5. How does Friar Francis feel about Hero's predicament? _____

Essay: Love is very important to everyone in this play. Tell about some different kinds of love which the characters show in the play. Give some examples showing how each character does or does not love.

Richard III

Richard III

Summary

In the very first lines of *Richard III*, Richard, the Duke of Gloucester, tells the audience who and what he is. Resentful because he was born gifted with high intelligence but cursed with gross physical abnormalities, he tells the audience in a fascinating soliloquy exactly what he thinks of himself, what he thinks of others, and how he intends to take the crown of England for himself through manipulation and trickery. In the remainder of the play, the audience watches Richard's schemes take fruit with the kind of fascination one would have watching a snake charmer manipulate a deadly snake.

Physically, Richard is a small man with a hunched back, crooked shoulders, poorly shaped limbs, and a hard-featured face. He has cultivated strong friendships through the years by seeming to be kind and generous, when in fact he would stop at nothing to get his own way. Unknown to the people he has befriended, he has manipulated and lied to make himself look good for them; and with an arrogance he acknowledges within himself, he has pretended to be friends with people he hates and intends to kill if they get in his way. He is evil, and he knows it and delights in it; but the other characters do not know it, and he is able to move them around like chessmen on a board. In a word, he is a sociopath—cunning, hateful, manipulative, and dangerous to all who cross his path. He has no conscience. Richard III is a monster.

The play begins with Richard telling the audience he is "determined to prove a villain." He first will destroy his brother Clarence by persuading King Edward IV to have him murdered, while he pretends to Clarence to be his friend. Next, Richard marries Anne, who is the daughter of the Earl of Warwick, whose husband and father he has murdered without her knowing about it. He is, however, in danger, for the King's relations hate him, and the widow of the former King, Henry VI, wanders in and out of the play prophesying woe to the enemies of the throne.

When King Edward is dying, Richard and his ally, Buckingham, seize the young Crown Prince and his brother and take them to the Tower of London, from which they never emerge. Then Richard quickly sets about to eliminate anyone he sees as an enemy, which is anyone loyal to Edward or his sons. One after another, they die—the "little princes," Lord Hastings, and Richard's wife, Anne. Suddenly the tide begins to turn against Richard as others begin to see him as he really is. Even Buckingham turns against him, and Richard orders his death.

Richard receives news that his enemies are rising up against him, and a civil war begins. Then on a dark night on the battlefield, the ghosts of Richard's victims rise up to confront him—Prince Edward, Henry VI, Clarence, Rivers, Vaughan, Grey, the two princes, Anne, Buckingham. The ghosts curse Richard, then disappear, and in the battle which follows, Richard is killed.

Sample Lesson Plans

Each of the lessons suggested below can take from one to several days to complete.

Lesson 1

❖ Introduce and complete some or all of the pre-reading activities found on pages 6–28.

❖ Read the play summary with your students (page 65).

❖ Generate the vocabulary list (ongoing during reading of the play) by having students skim quickly through Act I, jotting down words they do not know, then listing the words on the board.

❖ As a class, record meanings of words from footnotes or a dictionary into the class dictionary. Discuss the ways in which the meanings of words change over the years.

Lesson 2

❖ Read Act I, Scene i, aloud. As you read, place the vocabulary words in the context of the play.

❖ Do the vocabulary activities (page 27).

❖ Read "Who Was Richard III?" Discuss the fact that this play is a history and based on the deeds of a real king in England's history. (page 68)

❖ Read about the soliloquy, and translate one into modern English (pages 72–74).

❖ Write a character description of Richard based on his soliloquy.

❖ Create vocabulary words for Lesson 3.

Lesson 3

❖ Find meanings for vocabulary words, discuss them, and place them into the class dictionary.

❖ Read aloud Act I, Scenes ii through iv.

❖ Read about Shakespeare's London and complete the diagram showing contrasts and comparisons between London in Shakespeare's time and now (pages 69–71).

❖ Read about the Tower of London and its infamous past (pages 75–76).

❖ Build a model Tower, or design your own crown jewels (page 76).

❖ Generate vocabulary words for Act II.

Lesson 4

❖ Find meanings for vocabulary words for Act II. Discuss them and place them into the class dictionary.

❖ Read Act II aloud.

❖ Debate the idea that our consciences make cowards of us all (page 80).

❖ Learn about superstitions (pages 81–82).

❖ Take a superstitions survey.

❖ Generate vocabulary words for Act III.

Sample Lesson Plans *(cont.)*

Lesson 5

❖ Find the meanings for the vocabulary words for Act III. Discuss them and place them into the class dictionary.

❖ Read Act III aloud.

❖ Discuss the way Richard chooses to discredit the two princes and explain away their disappearance.

❖ Compile an almanac.

❖ Generate vocabulary words for Act IV.

Lesson 6

❖ Find meanings for the vocabulary words for Act IV. Discuss them and record them in the class dictionary.

❖ Read Act IV aloud.

❖ Rewrite the conversation between Queen Elizabeth and King Richard in Scene iv in modern English; then discuss its importance. What action is he about to undertake with his niece, and why is it so harshly received by the queen?

❖ Complete "Male or Female?" (page 86). Be prepared to give reasons for your choices.

❖ Generate vocabulary for Act V.

Lesson 7

❖ Find meanings for the vocabulary words for Act V. Discuss them and record them in the class dictionary.

❖ Read Act V aloud.

❖ Tell the story of Richard III from his perspective (page 88).

❖ Discuss the student's enjoyment of the play and any questions they have.

Lesson 8

❖ Administer the Section quiz (page 91).

❖ Assign and complete projects.

❖ Discuss corrected quizzes and answer questions regarding answers.

❖ Make plans for a culminating activity and choose committees.

Lesson 9

❖ Complete the culminating activity.

Who Was King Richard III?

King Edward IV of England died in 1483, leaving two sons, Edward V and the Duke of York; however, Edward, the elder heir to the throne, was only 12 years old. His uncle, Richard, Duke of Gloucester, promised the boy's father that he would protect the boy and keep him safe until he was old enough to rule; therefore, the dying king appointed Richard to rule as regent until the boy was grown. Shortly after the king died, Richard had both young princes taken to the infamous Tower of London, where he is said to have had them murdered and then had himself declared King Richard III of England.

Richard's actions caused great unrest among the nobility, and soon it was being whispered that the Earl of Richmond, who was living in exile, would be a better king than Richard. Many of the earl's backers left to join him in exile in France, where they began plotting with him to return to England and take the throne from Richard. In 1485, Henry, Earl of Richmond, landed in Wales, with 5,000 men; Richard III met him in battle at Market Bosworth west of Leicester. The earl's forces were greatly outnumbered by the 15,000 men who fought with Richard; however, some of Richard's forces waited to see how the battle would go before taking part in it.

Richard wanted to meet Henry personally in a hand-to-hand fight, but unluckily for him, the men who had supposedly been on Richard's side joined Henry on the battlefield. They surrounded Richard and killed him. His crown fell off and rolled into a thorn bush. Henry's men picked it up and put it on Henry's head, kneeling before him and declaring him to be king. Henry's last name was Tudor, and thus his ascent to the throne was the beginning of the era which came to be known as the Tudor period in England.

There was a rumor passed down for almost 200 years that Richard III had had the two little princes murdered in the Tower of London, for they were never seen alive outside the Tower once they were taken there. In 1674, the skeletons of two young boys were found under the floor at the foot of a staircase. Many people believe these skeletons to be the ones of the young boys who got in Richard's way when he wanted to take the throne. The remains of two skulls, thought to be those of the princes, are now in a stone urn in Westminster Abbey.

Activity

Research the Tudor period in England. How many kings and queens can you find who were Tudors, and when did the period end?

What is the last name of the present queen of England?

Can you find the Tudor style of architecture, which is popular today in both England and the United States?

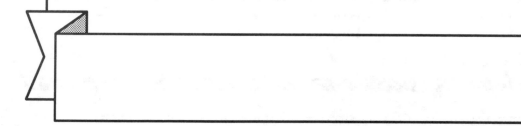

Elizabethan London

First built by the Romans almost 20 centuries ago, the London of Edward's and Elizabeth's time was a crowded complex of contrasts, most of it filthy and all of it smelly. A very small number of people were very rich and lived in grand homes, most of them outside the one square mile of urban London itself, for only the rich could afford to escape the stench of the streets. The poor were stuck in their misery.

There were many thousands of poor living in London. Some thought the reason they were poor was their own fault, that God was angry with them, or that they wasted what they had. It was also said they gambled and cursed and drank too much and even that they were wicked and did not go to church enough. Whatever the cause for their poverty, they usually remained poor until they died. There was a strong, strictly enforced code of class consciousness dividing the poor from the rich, and there was little chance of bettering oneself.

Most of London was destroyed by fire in 1666, but in the 1500s it was still crammed with small wooden houses which overhung the narrow lanes and were topped with wooden shingles. Even London Bridge was lined with houses and shops, and the pikes on the bridge were sometimes topped with the heads of those found guilty of various crimes, for the English justice system was high on retribution and low on mercy.

The Tower of London looked then much as it does now, its white keep rising alongside the Thames River. At ten o'clock each night the wind murmured ominously through the ancient trees inside the tower walls as the gates were locked in the same way they had been every night since the 1200s—with a ritual called the Ceremony of the Keys. To this day the rite has never failed to take place precisely on time each night, even during war. Elizabeth, the princess, heard the ancient rite from her cell when Bloody Mary was Queen; Sir Walter Raleigh heard it, as did the Earl of Essex. The 1800 people whose skeletons were found inside the chapel walls when Queen Victoria had it remodeled in the 1800s presumably heard it as well, along with Anne Boleyn (Elizabeth's mother), Lady Jane Grey, and the little princes imprisoned—some say murdered there—by King Richard III.

Westminster Palace no longer stands. It burned to the ground long ago and was replaced by the Houses of Parliament. Westminster Abbey still stands, however. Through all the political and religious turmoil which has rocked London over the centuries, the stone edifice has remained, gracefully accepting the changes in ritual which have taken place from the time when it was a Catholic monastery until now. It is one of the few truly ecumenical churches in the world, welcoming those of all religions who come to worship within its walls. Called a "royal peculiar," it does not fall under the authority of the Church of England except during the five months or so when it is being prepared to take its place as the site of coronation for England's kings and queens. It was there that Edward and Elizabeth were crowned.

Elizabethan London *(cont.)*

London's rich were very, very rich; and being rich meant having choices—choices about what to wear each day, what foods to eat, which wines to drink, which schools to attend, whether one would go on a cruise up the Thames when one wished, or go on a hunt. It meant being able to leave the city when the plague hit and being able to buy most of the pleasures in life, except freedom when one was incarcerated. To some extent, it even meant having a certain amount of power to control one's own destiny.

Being poor meant having no choices at all except which filthy pile of straw to sleep on at night in a room probably shared with many others. It meant getting no education, eating little food, none of it very healthy, wearing one set of clothes and, only if one was truly fortunate, owning one's own pair of shoes. If one lived in a small town and was deemed worthy, one might be able to have a small place of one's own in an alms house or "hospital," but in London that was out of the question. The poor were wretched, indeed—imprisoned within their poverty, condemned to spend their lives in narrow, filthy streets and small, cramped rooms.

Activities

1. Using the Venn diagram on page 71, compare and contrast the London of Shakespeare's time with the city in which you live. In space A, place symbols and words which describe Old London. In space C, place symbols and words which describe your city or town. And in space B, place symbols and words which describe characteristics which both cities share. Then write two or three paragraphs explaining your diagram.

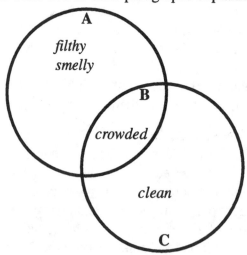

2. Draw a picture showing your idea of how London looked in Shakespeare's time; then draw one showing your city today. How are they different? Share your pictures with your classmates.

Venn Diagram

In space A, place symbols and words describing characteristics of Shakespeare's London. In space C, place symbols and words describing your city. In space B, place symbols and words showing characteristics which both cities share.

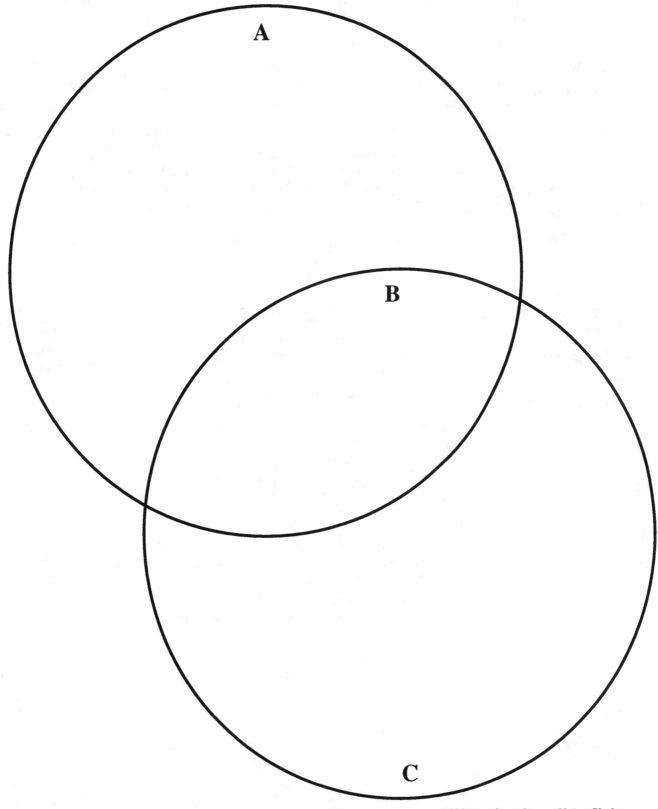

The Soliloquy

A speech in which a character tells his innermost thoughts is called a *soliloquy*. Read these two famous soliloquies. The first one is from the play *Hamlet*, which the young prince of Denmark (Hamlet) gives when he learns that his uncle has murdered Hamlet's father and then married his mother. The second is given by Richard III, telling the audience what kind of man he is. After reading them, choose one or more of the following activities.

1. Read the soliloquies carefully and then choose one and write a rendition of it in modern English. Do not try to render it word for word, because that might get you totally bogged down. Rather, write what you think the character is really thinking. What is he feeling when he says these words? What is he planning to do or thinking of doing?

2. Choose one of the soliloquies, and write a paragraph description of the character who speaks the lines. Use lines from the soliloquy to support your judgment of the character. What kind of person is he? How can you tell? Is he good or evil? Is he kind or gentle? Given what he says about himself, what do you think he looks like? Do you think his looks have anything to do with his outlook on life? Would you want to have this character for a friend? Why?

3. Memorize one of the soliloquies, or another one from a different play, and present it to the class.

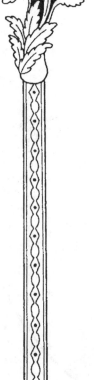

Hamlet's Soliloquy

Act III, Scene i

To be, or not to be—that is the question.
Whether 'tis nobler in the mind to suffer
The slings and arrows of outrageous fortune,
Or to take arms against a sea of troubles
And by opposing end them? To die: to sleep;
No more; and by a sleep to say we end
The heart-ache and the thousand natural shocks
That flesh is heir to, 'tis a consummation
Devoutly to be wish'd. To die, to sleep—
To sleep, perchance to dream. Ay, there's the rub,
For in that sleep of death what dreams may come
When we have shuffled off this mortal coil,
Must give us pause. There's the respect
That makes calamity of so long life.

The Soliloquy *(cont.)*

Hamlet's Soliloquy *(cont.)*

For who would bear the whips and scorns of time,
The oppressor's wrong, the proud man's contumely,
The pangs of despised love, the law's delay,
The insolence of office, and the spurns
That patient merit of the unworthy takes,
When he himself might his quietus make
With a bare bodkin? Who would fardels bear,
To grunt and sweat under a weary life,
But that the dread of something after death,
The undiscover'd country from whose bourn
No traveller returns, puzzles the will,
And makes us rather bear those ills we have
Than fly to others that we know not of?
Thus conscience does make cowards of us all,
And thus the native hue of resolution
Is sicklied o'er with the pale cast of thought,
And enterprises of great pith and moment
With this regard their currents turn awry,
And lose the name of action. —Soft you now!
The fair Ophelia! Nymph, in thy orisons
Be all my sins remember'd.

Soliloquy of Richard III

Act I, Scene i

Now is the winter of our discontent
Made glorious summer by this sun of York;
And all the clouds that low'r'd upon our house
In the deep bosom of the ocean buried.
Now are our brows bound with victorious wreaths;
Our bruised arms hung up for monuments;
Our stern alarums changed to merry meetings,
Our dreadful marches to delightful measures.
Grim-visaged war hath smoothed his wrinkled front,
And now, instead of mounting barded steeds
To fright the souls of fearful adversaries,
He capers nimbly in a lady's chamber
To the lascivious pleasing of a lute.

The Soliloquy *(cont.)*

Soliloquy of Richard III *(cont.)*

But I, that am not shaped for sportive tricks,
Nor made to court an amorous looking-glass;
I that am rudely stamp'd, and want love's majesty
To strut before a wanton ambling nymph;
I, that am curtail'd of this fair proportion,
Cheated of feature by dissembling nature,
Deformed, unfinish'd, sent before my time
Into this breathing world, scarce half made up,
And that so lamely and unfashionable
That dogs bark at me as I halt by them;
Why, I, in this weak piping time of peace,
Have no delight to pass away the time,
Unless to spy my shadow in the sun
And descant on mine own deformity,
And therefore, since I cannot prove a lover,
To entertain these fair well-spoken days,
I am determined to prove a villain
And hate the idle pleasures of these days.
Plots have I laid, inductions dangerous,
By drunken prophecies, libels and dreams,
To set my brother Clarence and the king
In deadly hate, the one against the other.
And if King Edward be as true and just
As I am subtle, false and treacherous,
This day should Clarence closely be mew'd up,
About a prophecy, which says that G
Of Edward's heirs the murderer shall be.
Dive, thoughts, down to my soul. Here Clarence comes.

The Tower of London

The Tower of London is one of the most famous (and infamous) buildings in the world. It was begun by William the Conqueror in 1078 as a castle and palace, and later it was enlarged to the size it is now. The Tower has been used for various purposes over the years, including an armory, a zoo, and a mint, but its most famous use was as a notorious prison.

The names of the people who were at one time or another locked within its stone walls read like a *Who's Who?* of English history, and include Sir Walter Raleigh, Mary Queen of Scots, Queen Elizabeth I when she was a princess, and Anne Boleyn, Elizabeth's mother. Some were imprisoned there for their religious beliefs. The kings and queens were so powerful that anyone they did not like or thought to be an enemy could be thrown in the Tower without a trial.

Many people were executed in the Tower, but the privilege of being beheaded was reserved for those who were of royal or noble blood, such as Anne Boleyn (who met with the displeasure of her husband, Henry VIII), Lady Jane Grey, who at 16 was queen for only nine days, and Sir Walter Raleigh. The block and axe used for a beheading in 1747 can be seen there now. People other than royalty or nobility who were judged to be criminal were subjected to worse fates than beheading if they were to be executed. The prisoners were all brought into the Tower by way of Traitor's Gate, which opens out to the Thames River.

The world's largest collection of jewels, the Crown Jewels of England, are kept in the Jewel House at the Tower. Huge receptacles for punch and dishes used to serve royal banquets were made of solid gold, and these may all be seen now in the Jewel House. Saint Edward's Crown, which is used for the coronation ceremony of a new monarch; the Imperial State Crown, which contains 3,000 precious jewels; and the biggest cut diamond in the world, the "Star of Africa," are all kept in the Jewel House.

The Tower of London *(cont.)*

The men who guard the Tower are officially called the Yeoman Warders, but are often called by the nickname "Beefeaters," a medieval term for well-fed servants. They may be recognized by their red, gold, and black uniforms. The men who serve as Yeoman Warders have all been highly decorated in the British armed forces. There are always 42 of them, and they are considered to have a very prestigious position; it is an honor to be named to the position. The governor, or superintendent, of the Yeoman Warders and the others live in the Tower, and they even have their own pub (short for "public house," but in this case more like an exclusive men's club) inside the walls.

The Tower is almost a small city within a city. There is even a chapel, or small church, which was built for the benefit of the prisoner's souls. This chapel is still in use, and visitors to London may attend services there any Sunday, except during August when the minister is on holiday. During the reign of Queen Victoria, the chapel was remodeled, and it is said that over 1,800 skeletons were found in the walls at that time. No one knows whose skeletons they were, however. Long ago, the royal zoo was kept in the Tower and included a polar bear which swam and fished in the moat which has since been drained. There is a group of other residents in the Tower even now—ravens. It is said that if the ravens ever disappear from the Tower, it will collapse. When a visitor looks at the Tower, it is difficult to imagine this happening, for it looks as solid as the Rock of Gibraltar.

The English enjoy the pomp and ceremony which goes with royalty and history, and a ceremony occurs in the Tower which has occurred each night without fail for over 700 years. It is called the Ceremony of the Keys, and it takes place at 10 o'clock when the Tower is locked up for the night. The time is adhered to exactly, and it is said that if it varied by even one second, the Yeoman Warder in charge would be fired immediately. To be one of those privileged to observe this solemn and historic ceremony is almost breathtaking, for one's mind is continually on the famous ancients whose souls may still be lurking on the grounds, and one continually wonders who those people were whose skeletons filled the walls. To add to the feeling of mystery one gets when watching the ceremony, just as the bell tolls ten a breeze often passes through the huge trees inside the wall, adding an eerie quality to the atmosphere.

Activities

1. Using a picture of the Tower of London, build a model of the Tower. What materials will you use?

2. Imagine that you have the most expensive and elaborate collection of jewels in the world. Draw a picture of your collection, and, if you choose, make a model of one or more of the items in your collection.

Writing About Literature

Some students enter school well-prepared to read and write the English language. These students come to school from a background where their parents or care-providers have surrounded them with English language books, magazines, and newspapers. They have spoken and heard the language all their lives. They have been read to in English regularly and have grown up in homes where high value has always been placed on education. They have come to school already equipped with a background of knowledge and language experiences which predict success in a school where the dominant language is English.

Many students entering schools today come with limited English skills. This happens for many different reasons. Some of these students come from homes in which a language other than English is spoken, so for a large part of their lives they have not been exposed to the nuances and shades of meaning in the very complex English language. Other students come with learning disabilities, and just learning the rudiments of reading and writing has taken much of their energy, leaving little to devote to the finer details of written English.

Other students come from homes where parents are so busy trying to provide the necessities of life they have not had the time or energy to provide their children with the necessary enriching language experiences. Others came from homes with parents who do not understand their part in the education of their children. At no other time in history has an attempt been made to educate all children, no matter what their backgrounds or disabilities, and sometimes it is necessary for teachers to employ new methods to teach all students.

The following approach to writing about literature has been very effective in teaching students with varying abilities from diverse backgrounds. It is highly structured and gives students a precise method to use when writing an expository essay. The method begins as a group activity, but once students learn it is possible to write by taking these steps, they can use it on their own.

Step by Step to Good Writing About Literature

1. **Ask a question.** After reading a piece of literature such as a chapter in a book, an act in a play, a short story, a poem, or a tale, pose a question to the students to which they are to write a response which comes from evidence in the play. Using Act I, scene i in *Richard III* as the piece of literature, the question could be this:

   How can the reader or playgoer know that Richard is ruthless and power hungry?

2. **Turn the question around** into a beginning sentence. Have all students write this sentence as the paragraph beginning (topic sentence).

   Example: *From the very beginning of Richard III, the playgoer can tell Richard is ruthless by what he tells the audience about himself.*

3. **Brainstorm things Richard says about himself** which show his ruthlessness and list the students' answers on the board. Point out that although Richard is dishonest and devious with the other characters in the play, he is very candid with the audience about what he intends to do and how he thinks. Model how to identify and select something from what Richard says to the audience to show what sort of person he is. These are examples of items which can be brainstormed and listed on the board. Accept all reasonable answers to the question.

   He is unhappy. ("Now is the winter of our discontent . . .")

   He doesn't like himself because of his physical handicaps. (Dogs bark at him when he walks by; considers himself deformed, half made-up, and unfashionable)

   He wants to be a villain. (He says, "I am determined to prove a villain.")

   He sets people against each other. (He caused the king to put his own brother in prison by lying about him.)

4. **After writing the topic sentence, use the evidence from the play** which the students have listed on the board to form the main body of the first paragraph. At this point, the students write their own versions of Richard's descriptions of himself following the topic sentence. They can use the evidence brainstormed, as well as other evidence they find, and make their own comments about it. Stress to the students that what they use must be written in complete sentences.

Step by Step to Good Writing About Literature *(cont.)*

5. **Write a wrap-up sentence** as a class which draws together or summarizes all of the information in the body of the paragraph.

   Example: *It is easy to see that Richard intends to get what he wants, and he does not care who he hurts in the process.*

6. **Sample paragraph:** Using the beginning and ending sentences and the brainstormed evidence, the first paragraph might look something like this.

   From the very beginning of Richard III, the playgoer can tell Richard is ruthless by what he tells the audience about himself. He says that he is discontented. He does not like himself and thinks he is so deformed and ugly even the dogs bark at him when he walks by. Richard wants to do bad things and has determined that he is going to be a villain. He has even turned the king against his own brother and influenced the king to throw Clarence into the Tower of London. It is easy to see that Richard intends to get what he wants, and he does not care who he hurts in the process.

Note: In teaching writing this way, the teacher needs to use his or her best judgment as to when students are able to write about literature without constant supervison. Include all the steps at the beginning. Some students or classes will be able to use the method by themselves after one demonstration. Others will need to follow the process with the teacher through several writing assignments.

Allow students who are ready to write independently to do so. For students who need more help, gradually withdraw one step at a time as they master a step. For example, have them supply their own summary sentence first. As they become more proficient, have them write their own topic sentence. Finally, have each student brainstorm his/her own supporting material for the main body.

Does Conscience Make Cowards?

In *Hamlet* the young prince says in his great soliloquy (page 73), "...conscience does make cowards of us all," and in *Richard III*, Shakespeare put almost the same words into the mouth of one of the men who have come to murder Clarence. In Act I, scene iv, the second murderer says, "It (conscience) is a dangerous thing—it makes a man a coward." He then goes on to talk about how conscience keeps a person from stealing or swearing and puts obstacles in the way of a person when that person begins to do something which is wrong.

Activity

Do you agree with the idea that having a conscience makes a person a coward because it prevents him from doing things he otherwise would do if he had none? Do you think that Shakespeare was trying to tell the audience it was bad to have a conscience?

Or, do you think he was saying that conscience is a necessary quality to have because that is what causes most people to refrain from doing things which are socially unacceptable? Why does Shakespeare put these words into the mouth of someone who is planning to kill another person?

In teams of three or four, debate this statement:

Shakespeare said that it was good to have no conscience.

To back up the position you take, use evidence from *Richard III*, as well as what you know about how the people of Shakespeare's England saw the world. When debating this question, consider how the people who act without a conscience ultimately end up.

Use the lines below to write notes and quotations from passages that support your views.

_____

_____

_____

_____

_____

_____

_____

_____

_____

_____

_____

_____

_____

Of Black Cats and Omens

The people of Shakespeare's time were very superstitious, and their superstitious beliefs often show up in his plays. These fearful beliefs led to all sorts of problems for anyone who was different in any way from the neighbors, because many times people became suspected of witchcraft just because they appeared strange to their neighbors. Below are some superstitions which were common during Shakespeare's time. Render these into modern English by reading them aloud. You will find that most of the words you will understand as soon as you hear them said. Discuss them, trying to understand what kinds of events could have produced such beliefs. Do you know of any modern superstitions which could have come from any of these?

❖ "How happily rose I on my right syde to day, or blessed me well, this happye or lucky day."

❖ "To finde a person drowned…Take a white loafe, and cast the same into the water, neer ye suspected place, and it wil forthwith goe directly ouer the dead body."

❖ "When witches wish to deprive a cow of milk, they beg a little of the milk or butter which comes from that cow; therefore women should take care, when they are asked by people suspected of this crime, not to give away the least thing to them. Women who, when they have been turning a churn to no purpose, and if they suspect some witch, procure butter from that witch. Then they make that butter into three pieces and throw them into the churn, invoking the Holy Trinity so all witchcraft is put to flight. The butter must be borrowed from the suspected witch."

❖ A witch living in Bury St. Edmunds, Suffolk, gave this advice to prevent one's horse from being stolen. "If you are willing to give your horse holy bread (Holy Communion bread) and holy water, your horse would not be stolen."

❖ "If a man dreams he sees bees fly into his house, that shall be the destruction of the house."

❖ "The entrance of a bee into a cottage is deemed a certain sign of death."

❖ In *Richard III*, when the ghost of Buckingham enters he says, "The Lights burne blew (blue). It is now dead midnight." This refers to the belief that if a candle burned blue, it was a sign there was a spirit in the house or not far from it.

❖ Witches often go about in the likeness of a cat. "When ye se a cat syt in a wyndowe in the sonne, & that she lyke her bodye, and that one of her fete be aboute her ey ye nede not doubte but yt shall rayne that daye."

❖ "To cure an ill caste by any Witch putt upon any childe, Take a childe so ill held & strike yt seven times on ye face & like upon ye navel with ye heart of a blacke cat; then roast ye heart and give of yt to eat seven nights at ye meale & yt shalle be well butt ye cate must be seven years olde & ye seventh dropped (born) at birth. Blood from such an heart laid to any witches dorepost or thrown over nighte upon her dorestep will cause a sore & great paine in her belly."

❖ "It is a very unfortunate thing for a man to meete early in a morning a blacke Cat."

❖ "It is most certaine that the breath and Sauour of cats destroy the lungs and in their beds have the aire corrupted and fall into fiver hectickes and consumptions."

❖ In *Romeo and Juliet* the speech "Good King of Cats, nothing but one of your nine lives" refers to the belief that cats have nine lives.

Of Black Cats and Omens *(cont.)*

Activity

Superstitions were very common during the time of Shakespeare because there were so many events and illnesses that people had no explanation for, and they needed to have answers for whatever troubled them. Today, with all the knowledge we have about science, the world, and the human body, many of the above superstitions would no longer be thought of as true. Nonetheless, some people still hold superstitions.

Ask your neighbors, teachers, friends, and family members whether they have any superstitions. Some might be about numbers or about the weather. Write down any you hear; then bring them to class and share them with your classmates. Do you think these beliefs are true?

Superstition Today

_____

_____

_____

_____

_____

_____

_____

_____

_____

_____

_____

_____

_____

_____

_____

Witches and Witch Hunts

Witches and a belief in witchcraft are generally supposed to have been accepted as facts of life by most people in Shakespeare's England, for that was a time when many people were executed as witches in England, Europe, and America. Nevertheless, there were many thinking people of that time who spoke out against the practice of witch hunting. One of the most famous works about witchcraft was *Discovery of Witchcraft*, published in 1584 by Reginald Scot.

Scot was very disturbed by the flimsy evidence which was used in the courts to convict people accused of being witches, so he researched the whole subject thoroughly in an attempt to show that the prosecution of witches was based on superstition and "erroneous novelties and imaginary conceptions." Many of the puritanical churchmen of the time condemned his work, citing phrases from the Bible to back up their beliefs that witches existed and were agents of the devil. Even the future king of England published his own book in 1597 to criticize Scot's book.

King James VI of Scotland, who would become King James I of England in 1603, was a religious man, and the version of the Bible published during his reign is still called the King James Version. James was very interested in witches and sometimes attended the examinations of people accused of witchcraft (in 1591 a number of Scottish people had been convicted of plotting to kill him by witchcraft). Popular accounts of that trial had been published in England in 1592, and Shakespeare is thought to have based the idea for the witches in *Macbeth* on some of those who had been convicted in this trial.

It is possible that some secret societies of witches did exist in Scotland and France, but there is no evidence that the practice of witchcraft was widespread in England. The ones who were convicted, however, were usually convicted of a murder by witchcraft, rather than just of being witches. Who were these unfortunate people?

According to Scot, most of the people accused of witchcraft were lonely and malicious old women:

> *lame, blear-eyed, pale, foul (smelly), and full of wrinkles; poor, sullen,*
> *superstitious, and papists (Roman Catholic); or such as know no*
> *religion: in whose drowsy minds the Devil hath gotten a fine seat; so*
> *as, what mischief, mischance, calamity, or slaughter is brought to*
> *pass, they are easily persuaded the same is done by themselves,*
> *imprinting in their minds an earnest and constant imagination thereof.*
> *They are lean and deformed, showing melancholy in their faces, to the*
> *horror of all that see them. They are doting, scolds, mad, devilish;*
> *and not much differing from them that are thought to be possessed*
> *with spirits.*

Witches and Witch Hunts *(cont.)*

In other words, the people accused of witchcraft, who were almost always women, were probably not guilty of anything more than being different from their neighbors and of being mentally ill, in addition to being disliked. It was a case where people who were a minority were unlike the majority of citizens, and who stood out because of their differences and were executed because of those differences. It was a way of getting rid of disagreeable people. A play written about witches was received by the people of Shakespeare's time much like a horror film is received today.

Few people today believe in witchcraft or that a person could kill another just by looking at him the wrong way, but the practice of witch hunting exhibited one characteristic which is unfortunately still around. That is the practice of discriminating against another person because of the way that person looks or because of other differences that person has.

Different people have different prejudices depending on their own physical makeup and upbringing. Some prejudices are based on how the disliked person looks, what he does, or what religion he practices which is different. These are called racial prejudices or religious prejudices. Sometimes people are prejudiced against those who are of a different social class or who look different because of some physical characteristic, such as a handicap. In any case, the person holding the prejudice bases his/her beliefs on the idea that the only good and acceptable people are like himself or herself. Most people have some prejudices, but when someone acts on his prejudices to deny equal treatment or to hurt another, it is no longer just prejudice. It becomes unfair discrimination.

Unfair discrimination takes many forms. It can be as subtle as not wanting to be seen in public with someone because of that person's ethnic background, gender, or religion. Or it can be as serious as keeping that person from getting the same education or job, harassing him, denying him access to services, or doing him physical harm.

In the United States it is unlawful to discriminate against another person based on that person's race, religion, age, gender, or ethnic background. Every U.S. citizen and anyone living in this country is protected by the U.S. Constitution. Those who discriminate against others can be tried and convicted if they abuse the civil rights of the target of the discrimination.

Witches and Witch Hunts *(cont.)*

Activity: You Be the Jury

In small groups, decide whether the action described is prejudice, discrimination, or neither. Then come together as a class and discuss the decisions you have made. Be prepared to defend your decisions.

Action	Prejudice	Discrimination	Neither
John does not like people who are a different color from him.			
The coach will not let Manny play on the team because of his religion.			
The male manager of a large business makes suggestive remarks to a young woman who works for him.			
Julie does not like Margaret because she belongs to a different religious group.			
A real estate salesperson does not show a house to a customer, because of that customer's race.			
At a large party, Arthur tells several jokes which make fun of people of color.			
When Bob, a Native American, gets on the school bus, several white students say, "How!" and laugh.			
James is a trained computer processor, but because he is in a wheelchair, the company does not hire him.			
Because she is 71 years old, Hattie Jones is not hired to work in a department store.			
Mike thinks everyone who goes to another church is evil.			
Joan makes fun of the new girl in school because she does not speak English very well.			

Male or Female?

Females were not allowed to act when Shakespeare was writing and producing his plays. This was true only in England, for in the rest of Europe women have been on the stage since playwriting began. Shakespeare's England had a large population of Puritans who thought that the theater was an instrument of the Devil and waged campaigns against it. This may or may not have had something to do with England's all-male plays. It did, however, result in the theaters being shut down altogether not too many years after Shakespeare's death. They did not reopen for several years. But while Shakespeare was alive, the theater was alive and well, and his acting company was supported by royalty, first by Queen Elizabeth I and then by King James I.

Female characters are in his plays, of course, but their parts were played by young men or boys. This certainly must have created some problems for the casting director or whoever decided what actor to put in a part. For one thing, a good female portrayer likely could not be one very long because he would outgrow his ability to play a realistic woman or girl. Can you imagine a boy whose voice was starting to change acting a girl's part? Or one with a bass voice? Having to cast boys as females may have been one reason Shakespeare's plays have many more male characters than female characters.

An interesting reversal of sorts is now happening in productions of Shakespeare's plays. Some male roles are being acted by females. For example, a recent production of *Hamlet* had females not only playing some of the smaller roles of squires and messengers, but a woman also played Rosencrantz, one of the conspirators usually collectively called Rosencrantz and Guildenstern. In this production, the pair were lovers. Not surprisingly, it worked, because many of Shakespeare's characters rely more on their characters and personalities than on their genders.

On the following page, decide whether or not the characters in the plays you have read could be played by someone of the opposite gender.

Male or Female? *(cont.)*

Which of the following female roles could be played today by males? Answer yes or no for each one and give the reason for your answer.

❖ Juliet _____

❖ Beatrice _____

❖ Hero_____

❖ Anne _____

❖ Juliet's nurse _____

❖ Margaret _____

❖ Ursula _____

Which of the following male roles could be played today by females? Answer yes or no for each one and give the reason for your answer.

❖ Benedick _____

❖ Romeo_____

❖ Don John_____

❖ Richard III_____

❖ Don Pedro _____

❖ Henry, Earl of Richmond _____

❖ Leonato _____

The Real Story According to Richard III

Shakespeare is pretty hard on Richard III. At the beginning of the play, he portrays Richard as a complete villain, and for the remainder of the play, he tells you only things which will prove what he has already told you. The only words he writes into Richard's mouth are those which show him to be a liar, a manipulator, and a murderer.

Have you ever heard the story from the point of view of Richard? No.

If Richard were on trial, by now he would have been "convicted by the media," and no one would ever have known what really happened.

Pretend you have been named public defender for Richard III. Now is your chance to intercede for Richard and to tell his story as he sees it. Write Richard's story in the space below.

Richard's Defense

_____

_____

_____

_____

_____

_____

_____

_____

_____

_____

_____

_____

Journal Questions

Use these questions for journals or for class discussions.

Act I

❖ How does Richard feel about himself, and how can you tell?

❖ Do you think the way he feels about himself affects the way he feels about others?

❖ Who is Richard's first victim, and what happens to him?

❖ What plans does Richard set for Lady Anne?

❖ Why do others not see what Richard is doing?

❖ How does Richard make sure that Clarence is executed?

Act II

❖ Why is the king surprised that Clarence is dead?

❖ Who is the next to die after Clarence?

❖ What does the queen mean when she says, "Pitchers have ears?"

❖ Why were Lord Rivers and Lord Grey sent to Pomfret, and what did that mean?

Act III

❖ Why did the brother of the young prince meet them in London?

❖ How does Richard get the young princes to the Tower?

❖ What does Richard say he will do if Lord Hastings does not do what he wants him to do? What actually happens?

❖ How does Richard explain this?

❖ What does Richard tell Buckingham to say about the two young princes?

❖ Why does Richard first say "No" when Buckingham says Richard should become king?

Act IV

❖ Why is the Duchess so unhappy that she calls her womb "the bed of death"?

❖ Where does Richard seat himself?

❖ What is Richard planning for his wife, the former Lady Anne? And what is he planning next for himself?

❖ What is Richard's first deed as king?

❖ Where have Buckingham, Richmond, and Ely gone?

Act V

❖ What ghosts appear to Richard, and what do they tell him?

❖ What did Richard mean by "coward conscience"?

❖ Why is Richard going to war?

❖ How does Richard describe his enemy to his troops?

❖ Why does Richard offer to give up his kingdom for a horse?

❖ How did Richard finally end up?

Responses

Explain the meanings of the following lines from *Richard III*.

1. "Now is the winter of our discontent made glorious summer by this sun of York."

   _____

   _____

2. "Simple, plain Clarence! I do love thee so
   That I will shortly send thy soul to Heaven."

   _____

   _____

3. "I'll have her, but I will not keep her long."

   _____

   _____

4. "Out, devil! I remember them too well.
   Thou slewest my husband Henry in the Tower,
   And Edward, my poor son, at Tewksbury."

   _____

   _____

5. "A man cannot steal but it accuseth him."

   _____

   _____

6. "So wise so young, they say, do never live long."

   _____

   _____

7. "The tyrannous and bloody deed is done,
   The most arch act of piteous massacre
   That ever yet this land was guilty of."

   _____

   _____

8. "Why, then All Soul's Day is my body's Doomsday."

   _____

   _____

9. "God and our good cause fight upon our side."

   _____

   _____

10. A horse! A horse! My kingdom for a horse!"

   _____

   _____

Objective Test and Essay

Matching: Match the descriptions of the characters with their names.

1. King Edward IV   _____   A. Queen to King Edward IV

2. Lady Anne   _____   B. Lieutenant of the Tower of London

3. Earl of Richmond   _____   C. Tricked into executing Clarence

4. Richard III   _____   D. Widow of the Prince of Wales; marries Richard III

5. Duke of York   _____   E. Friend of the king who was betrayed by him

6. Prince of Wales   _____   F. Became Henry VII

7. Cardinal Bourchier   _____   G. Has no conscience

8. Buckingham   _____   H. Shut up in the Tower

9. Brakenbury   _____   I. Archbishop of Canterbury

10. Elizabeth   _____   J. Shut up in the Tower

True or False: Answer true or false in the blanks below.

1. _____ The Duke of Gloucester had himself crowned king.

2. _____ Lady Anne had always been in love with Richard.

3. _____ The young Prince of Wales was sent to school by his Uncle Richard.

4. _____ Many ghosts appear to Richard.

5. _____ *Richard III* tells about a good king who did much for his people.

Short Answer: Write a brief response to each question in the space provided.

1. Where does *Richard III* take place? _____

2. What does Richard offer to give up his kingdom for? _____

3. What does Richard plan to do to his wife? _____

4. Describe the place where the two young princes went. _____

5. Name three people Richard betrayed. _____

Essay: Richard was willing to do anything to get what he wanted. Describe what means he took to get power and give the reasons you think he did these things.

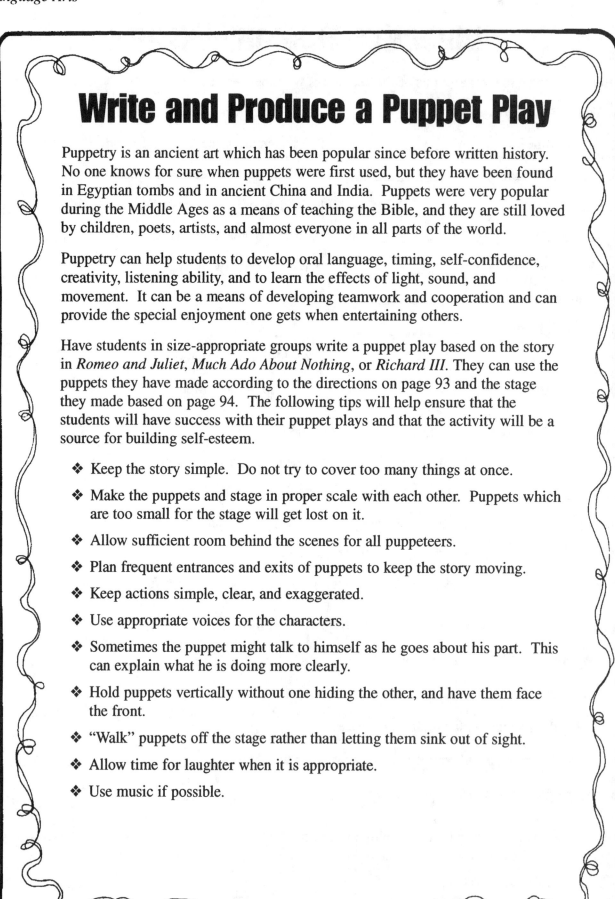

Write and Produce a Puppet Play

Puppetry is an ancient art which has been popular since before written history. No one knows for sure when puppets were first used, but they have been found in Egyptian tombs and in ancient China and India. Puppets were very popular during the Middle Ages as a means of teaching the Bible, and they are still loved by children, poets, artists, and almost everyone in all parts of the world.

Puppetry can help students to develop oral language, timing, self-confidence, creativity, listening ability, and to learn the effects of light, sound, and movement. It can be a means of developing teamwork and cooperation and can provide the special enjoyment one gets when entertaining others.

Have students in size-appropriate groups write a puppet play based on the story in *Romeo and Juliet, Much Ado About Nothing,* or *Richard III.* They can use the puppets they have made according to the directions on page 93 and the stage they made based on page 94. The following tips will help ensure that the students will have success with their puppet plays and that the activity will be a source for building self-esteem.

❖ Keep the story simple. Do not try to cover too many things at once.

❖ Make the puppets and stage in proper scale with each other. Puppets which are too small for the stage will get lost on it.

❖ Allow sufficient room behind the scenes for all puppeteers.

❖ Plan frequent entrances and exits of puppets to keep the story moving.

❖ Keep actions simple, clear, and exaggerated.

❖ Use appropriate voices for the characters.

❖ Sometimes the puppet might talk to himself as he goes about his part. This can explain what he is doing more clearly.

❖ Hold puppets vertically without one hiding the other, and have them face the front.

❖ "Walk" puppets off the stage rather than letting them sink out of sight.

❖ Allow time for laughter when it is appropriate.

❖ Use music if possible.

92

Puppets: The Actors Therein

Puppets can be made with almost any material, from paper bags and old socks to the elaborate and expensive custom creations which a professional puppeteer might wish to have. One way to make puppets is to represent your characters with heads made from Styrofoam balls, sponges, sheets of polyfoam, or cloth. A favorite material to use for the puppet heads is papier-mâché because it is light, easy to work with, inexpensive, can easily be molded into various shapes, and can be painted in any manner you wish.

To make a papier-mâché puppet you will need the following:

❖ A bowl or round object about 5–6 inches (12.5–15 cm) in diameter

❖ Liquid soap or petroleum jelly

❖ Torn newspaper strips

❖ Wallpaper paste

❖ Paint

❖ Various objects and pieces of cardboard suitable for forming features

❖ Glue

❖ Craft stick or wooden dowel for holder

Directions:

1. Apply a thin coat of soap or petroleum jelly to the bowl.

2. Mix wallpaper paste to a thick liquid.

3. Tear newspaper strips about 1 to 1 $\frac{1}{2}$ inches (2.5–4 cm) wide.

4. Dip strips into the paste and run through fingers to remove excess.

5. Lay strips over the greased or soaped bowl, overlapping them in different directions. Apply two layers, letting each layer dry before applying another.

6. Add a framework for facial features such as nose, eyes, etc.

7. Glue the stick to bottom of the face for a holder.

8. Cover the entire face with one or two additional layers of paper strips until it looks the way you want it to look. Let dry.

9. Paint your puppet and set it in a safe place to dry.

And there you have it!

Make Your World a Stage!

Puppet theaters have been around for hundreds, probably even thousands, of years. "Punch and Judy" is one of the most famous pairs of puppets, and puppets of many kinds are very popular in all parts of the world. It is fun and really quite simple to make your own theater.

For a tabletop theater you will need the following:

❖ A large cardboard box at least 24 inches (60 cm) high

❖ Scissors

❖ Poster paints

❖ Fabric for curtains if desired

Directions:

1. Cut out the back of the box.

2. Cut an opening in front of the box. Leave a "frame" of at least four inches (10 cm) all around.

3. Decorate as you like. You might even try applying some papier–mâché "carving."

4. Cut and sew curtains if you wish to have them.

5. Set your new stage on a table covered with a black, floor-length skirt.

Comedy and Tragedy

The masks shown on this page are similar to ones used for thousands of years to designate two of the principal forms of drama: comedy and tragedy. As you can see, the masks are basically alike except that one shows an upturned mouth and downturned eyes to indicate laughter, and the other shows a downturned mouth and upturned eyes to indicate sadness. Just as these masks are very similar, so Shakespeare's comedy and tragedy are somewhat alike in plot, except that comedy ends happily, and tragedy unhappily.

An example of Shakespearean tragedy is *Romeo and Juliet.* Romeo and Juliet meet, fall in love, get married; and then, because one of them receives misinformation, both lovers end up dead. In *Much Ado About Nothing,* two lovers are prevented from marrying at first because one receives misinformation, but the error is discovered by the lovers in time for the wedding to take place after all, with the assumption that the lovers will live happily ever after.

The line between comedy and tragedy can be very fine, indeed. One needs only to watch a good Charlie Chaplin movie to realize this. Truly good comedy can come very close to being truly sad, with the difference being that all comes out okay in the end. Even Shakespeare's greatest tragedies contain "comic relief." The gravedigger scene in *Hamlet* is an example: Two gravediggers laugh and joke about life while digging the burial place for someone's dead body.

Decide whether each of the following basic plots is a comedy or tragedy:

1. Falstaff sets out to deceive two merry wives by pretending to be in love with them, but they outwit him and teach the husband of one a lesson at the same time.

   Comedy or Tragedy—Explain: _____

   _____

2. Falstaff spends a hilarious time with young Prince Henry, carousing in taverns and having a good time, but Henry is using Falstaff for his own ends until the time Henry will take the throne as king.

   Comedy or Tragedy—Explain: _____

   _____

3. Four young gentlemen form a scholarly academy and vow that for three years they will stay away from women, partying, and too much sleep, but they meet four young gentlewomen who end up getting marital promises from them.

   Comedy or Tragedy—Explain: _____

   _____

4. A young prince decides to seek revenge for the death of his dead father, and in doing so causes the madness of his beloved girlfriend and then becomes mad himself.

   Comedy or Tragedy—Explain: _____

   _____

Shakespeare Word Search

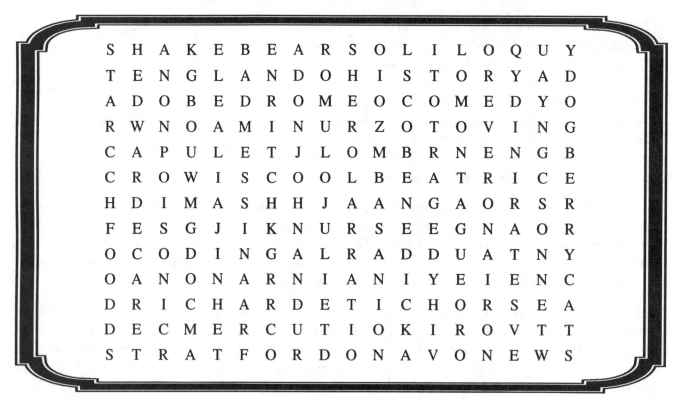

```
S H A K E B E A R S O L I L O Q U Y
T E N G L A N D O H I S T O R Y A D
A D O B E D R O M E O C O M E D Y O
R W N O A M I N U R Z O T O V I N G
C A P U L E T J L O M B R N E N G B
C R O W I S C O O L B E A T R I C E
H D I M A S H H J A A N G A O R S R
F E S G J I K N U R S E E G N A O R
O C O D I N G A L R A D D U A T N Y
O A N O N A R N I A N I Y E I E N C
D R I C H A R D E T I C H O R S E A
D E C M E R C U T I O K I R O V T T
S T R A T F O R D O N A V O N E W S
```

Clues

In this word search, find the names which identify the persons, places, or things in the clues.

1. A man with no conscience
2. Friend of Romeo
3. Likens Romeo to the stars
4. Claims to hate Benedick
5. Confuses people when he talks
6. A formal poem with 14 lines
7. Romeo's family name
8. Villain out to get Claudio
9. Scene of great romance and tragedy
10. Loved and cared for Juliet since she was a baby
11. Stands under a balcony to soliloquize
12. Young Prince of Wales killed by Richard III
13. Insults Beatrice to her face
14. Family name of Juliet
15. Country in which Richard III takes place
16. Sweet girl slandered by a villain
17. Scene of *Much Ado About Nothing*
18. What Juliet takes
19. What Richard calls for
20. A play about something which really happened
21. A play ending with a dramatic and disastrous event
22. A humorous play which ends happily
23. A speech in which a character reveals what he is thinking

Using Active Verbs

Shakespeare's plays are filled with action, and the playgoer watching a Shakespeare play learns as much about a character by the actions he takes as by the words he speaks. Action is important in writing prose and poetry. Adjectives, or words that describe nouns, can be very useful when writing a description of a person, but sometimes they can be a little boring to read. Another kind of word may describe a person better than an adjective—that word is the *active verb*.

Active verbs are words which show action. The best ones for writing show specific actions. Take, for example, the action word "walk." There are many different words which mean specific kinds of walking, and the descriptive picture you get in your head when you read each one is different from the picture you get when you read another. Do you get any particular idea of the kind of action the girl is taking in this sentence?

> The beautiful girl walked across the crowded room.

How does the picture change when you substitute another word for "walk" in these sentences?

> The beautiful girl *strolled* across the crowded room.
> The beautiful girl *dashed* across the crowded room.
> The beautiful girl *glided* across the crowded room.

Each of these sentences has a synonym for walk as a verb, yet by changing only that verb, you have changed the entire meaning of the sentence. The first sentence is vague, and you do not get a clear picture of the girl. When the word "danced" is used, you see a happy person joyfully crossing the room. With the word "dashed," you see someone in a hurry, and with "glided" you see a beautiful girl who almost floats, who moves lightly and gracefully.

Activity

1. List all the active words you can think of to use instead of these: *talk, help, fight, hold.* Now write a sentence with each of the words you have listed. How are these sentences clearer than a sentence using one of the four words above? Are you able to see a person in action better by using a different verb?

_____

_____

_____

_____

_____

_____

_____

_____

2. Following this activity, solve the active verb crossword puzzle.

Active Verb Crossword Puzzle

Word List

Appeared

Blazed

Burst

Commandeth

Cowered

Crashed

Exchanged

Fell

Fidgeted

Flew

Hesitated

Infuriated

Mumbled

Offend

Pressed

Reeled

Signified

Struggle

Threaded

Touched

Twitch

Whispered

Across

3. Lord Hertford _____ to Tom.
4. The party _____ suddenly out of darkness.
6. This speech _____ the swine.
9. The two lords _____ glances.
12. Tom _____ something.
13. He touched a bell and a page _____ .
14. Hertford _____ to him to make a sign.
16. The palace _____ with light.
19. His cudgel _____ down upon the meddler's head.
20. Miles _____ .
21. Two frowsy girls and a woman _____ against the wall.
22. Tom _____ from the blow.

Down

1. The muscles of his nose began to_____.
2. He_____ a bell and a page appeared.
5. Our friends _____ their way through the throngs.
7. The mother _____ on her knees before the prince.
8. Tom _____ assent with a gesture.
10. Lord St. John said, "His majesty _____."
11. The prince continued to _____ for freedom.
15. The constable _____ and spat out an oath.
17. The mob _____ on.
18. The prince said, "_____ me not with thy sordid matters."

Produce a Morality Play

The people in England had loved drama for centuries before Shakespare began writing his plays, and it is recorded that when Shakespeare was a child, traveling actors had been invited to Stratford-upon-Avon by his father who was prominent in the local government. The plays he would have seen were probably of the kind called *morality plays*.

Morality plays began during the Middle Ages as religious plays put on by the Church. Most people could not read or write, so the churchmen first set up scenes with monks portraying the characters intended to teach the people about the Bible. Then the monks began to act out the scenes which a storyteller explained. After awhile, the actors began to speak lines and make up material which was not in the Bible. Of course, the ultimate purpose of the plays, as the term "morality play" suggests, was to warn the people how to live correctly, go to church, pay tithes, and follow the Church's teachings. Some of the most popular plays had graphic descriptions of sinners being thrown to hell.

As the centuries passed, audiences liked the plays more and more until it became no longer possible for them to be held inside the church. The actors began producing their plays outside the churches at various places around the towns. Groups of people called *guilds* began to each act out their own parts of the story, moving around the town on movable stages called *pageants*. By the time Shakespeare began writing plays, they no longer were connected with the Church, and, in fact, some Protestant clergymen strenuously objected to them as being sinful and tried to prevent them.

Activity: In groups of four or five, write and produce a morality play. Choose a story which shows how those who fail to do the right thing end up being punished. Write your dialogue and design your scenery; then produce your play for the rest of the class.

Write Like a Pro

Being able to write clearly and well is a skill which is increasingly important to learn as more and more people find they must write reports and fill out forms as part of their jobs. Some people think that the ability to write is something only a few are born with and that it is impossible to learn unless one has a natural talent for it. This simply is not so.

Anyone who speaks and understands language can learn to write, but it takes practice and a willingness to look at your own work with a critical eye to see whether you have followed certain guidelines of good writing. The checklist at the bottom of this page can be useful when writing and rewriting your papers.

To get an understanding of how this checklist can help you, write a paper on a topic suggested by your teacher, and then use the checklist to evaluate your paper. Pretend the paper was written by someone else, and ask yourself, "Can I say yes to each of these questions about this paper?" Be honest. If you can say yes to most, or all, of the questions, you are well on your way to writing like a professional. Make any changes you need to make.

Writer's Checklist

	Yes	No
❖ Is my first sentence strong? Does it make someone want to read on?	_____	_____
❖ Have I used strong, active verbs?	_____	_____
❖ Have I avoided unnecessary adjectives and instead used active verbs to give a better picture of what I want to say?	_____	_____
❖ Have I avoided the use of taboo words which do not say anything, words such as *nice, sad, pretty, ugly, good, bad,* etc., and used more precise words or examples instead?	_____	_____
❖ Have I written complete sentences?	_____	_____
❖ Have I written my most important points first and used later ones to support what I want to say?	_____	_____
❖ Have I written short paragraphs which lead from one to the next in a manner which is easily read?	_____	_____
❖ Have I written a final sentence which brings closure to my paper?	_____	_____
❖ Have I remembered that anything I write will be read by someone else and therefore must be clear?	_____	_____

Saying It Like Shakespeare

Someone once said that he liked reading Shakespeare because it was so full of quotes. It is true that no other author has contributed to the language as many original lines and phrases as he did. In fact, Bartlett's book, *Familiar Quotations,* contains 88 pages of quotations from Shakespeare, many more than any other writer; actually, many of these sayings were created by Shakespeare.

Here are some of the better-known phrases:

- ❖ "Household words" *(Henry V)*
- ❖ "Neither rhyme nor reason" *(The Comedy of Errors)*
- ❖ "The primrose path" *(Hamlet)*
- ❖ "Laughing-stock" *(The Merry Wives of Windsor)*
- ❖ "Eaten me out of house and home" *(Henry IV, Part II)*
- ❖ "What the dickens!" *(The Merry Wives of Windsor)*
- ❖ "Foregone conclusion" *(Othello)*
- ❖ "One fell swoop" *(Macbeth)*
- ❖ "Hoodwinked" *(All's Well That Ends Well)*
- ❖ "The apple of her eye" *(Love's Labour's Lost)*
- ❖ "Sweets to the sweet" *(Hamlet)*
- ❖ "Too much of a good thing" *(As You Like It)*
- ❖ "The game is up" *(Cymbeline)*
- ❖ "The naked truth" *(Love's Labour's Lost)*
- ❖ "Knock, knock! Who's there?" *(Macbeth)*
- ❖ "For goodness sake" *(Henry VIII)*
- ❖ "What fools these mortals be!" *(A Midsummer Night's Dream)*
- ❖ "Star-crossed lovers" *(Romeo and Juliet)*
- ❖ "Good riddance" *(Troilus and Cressida)*

How many of these sayings have you heard? (A better question might be, how many have you **not** heard?)

Activity

Write a story in which you use as many of these quotes as possible. Your story can be as silly as you wish it to be, so have fun! Can you write a story in which you use all of these sayings?

Weights and Measures

Can you imagine how it would be if there were no standard weights and measures? If you asked for a liter of soda, you might get one amount in Store A and a different amount, more or less, in Store B. When you asked for anything, you would not know how much of it you were going to get until you got it. If the store clerk liked another customer better than he liked you, he might give that person more for the same amount of money, and you would not be able to do anything about it. That is how it was during the Middle Ages when each town had its own set of weights and measures.

During the reign of Queen Elizabeth I, the English government decided to see that weights and measures were the same all over England, and in 1588 it made enough sets of standard weights and measures for every city and town in the country. These standards might seem a little primitive to most of us who have become accustomed to computerized scales which measure everything down to a microscopic amount or length.

There was a brass rod to measure a yard and containers which measured a pint, a quart, a gallon, and a bushel. The bushel, also known as a "strike," held eight gallons and was intended to measure grain, not liquids. These standards were kept in the town hall, and occasionally a group of 12 men known to be honest used them to check the weights and measures of the town merchants. If a farmer thought he was being cheated, he could complain to the government. Penalties for under-measuring were usually severe, and the cheating storekeep might earn himself a stay in the stocks.

Activity

The weights and measures used in the United States were, until recently, based on the old English (or Imperial) standards. When the metric measuring standards based on the decimal system and used in most of the rest of the world were introduced to the American public, many Americans resisted the change, and most products continue to be labeled according to both systems. A typical box of sugar, for example, will be labeled "32 oz. (2 lbs.) 907 g," and as a general rule, cooking recipes still call for the cups, tablespoons, and teaspoons of the old English system. Despite resistance to it, the metric system is easy. Using this approximate conversion chart, convert the old English amounts to metric.

Equivalents

❖ 1 quart = 1 liter

❖ 1 tablespoon = 15 milliliters

❖ 1 cup = 250 milliliters

❖ 1 pound = 480 grams

❖ 1 inch = 2.5 centimeters

Convert these to metric measures.

1. 2 gallons _____
2. 5 pints_____
3. 15 cups _____
4. 3 tablespoons _____
5. ½ cup _____
6. 5 tablespoons _____
7. 7 cups _____
8. 1½ pints _____

9. 4 quarts _____
10. 3 pounds_____
11. ¼ pound _____
12. 1 ton _____
13. 1 foot _____
14. 6 inches _____
15. 1 yard _____

Theater Math

During his time in London, Shakespeare himself owned a share of the Globe theater and was a good businessman, retiring by the time he was 50. He was very aware of attendance figures and profits. If he were alive and in the entertainment business today, he would be quite at home dealing with the following problems.

The Pantages Theater in Umberto, California, showed the following statistics for March 1957:

- ❖ Total number of tickets sold 5,687
- ❖ Of the total, senior citizens bought 1,645
- ❖ Of the total, juniors bought 1,598

1. General admission customers bought the rest of the tickets sold. How many were there?_____

2. What percentage of tickets was sold to senior citizens? _____

3. What percentage of tickets was bought by juniors? _____

4. In April, the theater showed a movie which proved to be very popular. Total senior citizen receipts for that month was approximately 257% of those in March. How many seniors bought tickets in April? _____

5. In April, junior ticket receipts were 4,258. What percentage of March receipts was this?_____

6. General admission customers in April bought 3,492 tickets. How many tickets were sold altogether in the month of April? _____

7. Encouraged by the gain in ticket sales in April, the theater manager set a goal of 12,000 tickets to be sold in May. How many more tickets would this be than were sold in March?_____ What percentage of tickets sold in March would this be? _____

8. A flu epidemic hit Umberto in the month of May, however, and the number of tickets sold was 58% of the tickets sold in March. How many senior tickets were sold? How many junior tickets were sold? How many general admission tickets were sold? _____

A theater often makes more of its income on the popcorn, sodas, and food items sold at its concession stand than it does on tickets. Calculate the following:

9. On each box of popcorn sold, the theater made a profit of 91%. If 1,395 boxes of popcorn were sold at an average of $2.50 each, how much profit did the theater make on popcorn? _____

10. If each soda costs the theater $.34, and it sells the sodas for $1.50, how much profit will the theater make . . .

  A. on each soda? _____

  B. on each 100 sodas? _____

  C. on each 592 sodas? _____

  What percentage profit will the theater make on sodas?_____

Elizabethan Money

English money during Shakespeare's time was complicated when compared to American or English money today. Today's money is decimalized—that is, it is based on units of ten, so we have the following:

❖ 100 pennies = 1 dollar

        or

❖ 100 pence = 1 pound

Decimalizing the money made it much easier to add, subtract, multiply, and divide in terms of prices, costs, profits, etc. English money during Shakespeare's time, however, was not decimalized, so figuring it out sometimes took a lot of work. The following may give an indication of just what was involved in trying to solve a problem using money.

❖ 12 pennies (12 d) = 1 shilling (1 s)
❖ 20 shillings (20 s) = 1 pound (1 £)

To make it more difficult, there were other coins, such as these:

❖ halfpenny, called "ha penny" ($\frac{1}{2}$ d)
❖ farthing ($\frac{1}{4}$ d), which was one-fourth of a penny
❖ mark, which was $\frac{2}{3}$ of a pound (or 13 s-4 d).

Then there were half marks, 3/4 shillings, threepence, and so on. If you want to change old English money into new, the easiest way to estimate would be to multiply the number of shillings by five to get an answer in new pence, or you can count 2.4d as one new penny. Since old pennies, halfpennies, and farthings would be worth next to nothing now, it is probably best just to ignore them altogether. Of course, if you want to convert English pounds into American dollars, you have to watch the nightly business news to see just what the current exchange rate of pounds for dollars is; and if you are trying to exchange dollars for pounds, or vice versa, you will need to include the fee charged by the bank for that service.

(Actually, when you get right down to it, you are probably better off just to forget the whole thing—or trust the bank teller to figure it out for you!)

Noble Budgeting

How a Nobleman Got His Money

Noblemen were men who had inherited wealth and property and were, therefore, able to wield a lot of power over the people who lived on their lands. The most important of the ways in which the noblemen wielded power was in their control over the money made on and by their lands. They themselves did not work the land. Tenants rented the lands from the lord, generally paying him both in money and in produce. In this way, no matter where the lord was or what he was doing, money continued to pour into his coffers, and all he had to do was manage it and spend it.

Below is a budget showing the income and expenses of a fictional noble called the Earl of Wakering. Use the budget to answer the questions at the bottom of the page.

Income—January 1 to July 31, 1592

Money won by his Lordship at gambling	550 £
Incoming rents (paid yearly)	6,100 £
Fines (money paid to noble by tenant when taking over a farm)	1,600 £
Sales of firewood	1,400 £
Money borrowed	2,350 £
Total	**12,000 £**

Expenses—January 1 to July, 1592

Bread (296 loaves from baker)	£15-6s-0d
Beer (56 barrels from brewer)	£15-16s-10d
Meat (beef, mutton, and veal from butcher)	£353-23s-15d
Stable charges	£247-6s-9d
Horsehoeing	£15-4s-5d
Falconers and hawks	£67-12s-2d
Hound keeper	£12-3s-7d
Household necessities (pots, andirons, etc.)	£51-4s-3d
New crossbow	£2-5s-2d
Eight oyster knives	£4s-2d
Alms (paid to Church for the needy)	£15
Rewards (tips to service people)	£176
Jewelry	£1,246
Debts	£1,700

Discussion Questions

1. How much did the nobleman pay in taxes?
2. What items are listed on this budget that probably would not be in one for your family?
3. What are the three biggest expenses on the nobleman's budget?
4. What was the source of most of his income?
5. How much did the nobleman spend for fruits and vegetables?
6. What can you tell about the life of a nobleman by reading this budget?

Plague Percentages

Several different deadly diseases hit England in huge waves before, during, and after the time of Shakespeare. The most infamous of these diseases was the bubonic plague, sometimes called the "Black Death." Using the chart on page 108 showing the list of people killed by all diseases in the year 1593, answer the following:

1. List in correct 1,2,3 order the three months in which the largest number of people died from...

    A. all diseases: _____   _____   _____

    B. the plague: _____   _____   _____

2. Using the totals at the bottom of the chart, what percentage of total deaths from diseases did the plague account for? _____

3. If 250,000 people lived in London during 1593, what percentage of them died from...

    A. various diseases?_____

    B. the plague? _____

4. If all the students in your class were alive in 1593, how many of them would have died from...

    A. various diseases?_____

    B. the plague? _____

5. Usually, death rates are given per thousand. For example, if the death rate is 12 per thousand, that means 12 of every 1,000 people died. What would be the death rate if 25,000 of the 250,000 residents of London died in 1593? _____

6. How many people died of the plague in the month of August 1593? _____
   What percentage was that of the total deaths caused by disease in August? _____

7. How many people died of the plague in July 1593? _____ What percentage of the total deaths from disease was that? _____

8. What reasons can you think of for the much higher numbers of people dying from all diseases during July, August, and September? _____

    _____

    _____

    for the numbers of people dying from the plague during these months? _____

    _____

    _____

Converting Celsius to Fahrenheit

If you stand in the sunshine, you will feel warm. If you play a fast game of soccer, you will feel hot. Just as the sun generates heat, your body also produces heat all the time, and it is this heat which keeps you alive. Sometimes when your body produces more heat than usual (as it does when you have a fever), your temperature can be measured by an instrument called a thermometer.

The first thermometer for measuring temperature was invented by Galileo in 1596, while Shakespeare was in London, but a thermometer was not used to measure human temperature until 1626. Almost 90 years later, in 1714, Gabriel D. Fahrenheit constructed a mercury thermometer on which there was a temperature scale. In 1742 the Swiss astronomer, Anders Celsius, invented the centigrade thermometer.

Scientists (and most of the world) now use the centigrade thermometer, measuring heat in centigrade degrees called "degrees Celsius." However, in the United States heat is still measured by Fahrenheit as well as centigrade degrees, and weather reporting is still done in Fahrenheit degrees. When Americans travel to other countries, they sometimes are confused by weather reporting on radio and television because weather temperatures are reported in Celsius degrees only.

If you travel abroad, how can you convert Celsius degrees to Fahrenheit degrees to get an understanding of what to expect of the weather? Remember the following facts:

1. On the Fahrenheit scale, water freezes at 32 degrees and boils at 212 degrees.

2. On the Celsius scale, water freezes at 0 degrees and boils at 100 degrees. One degree Fahrenheit is one and four-fifths degrees Celsius, but the scales start at a different base. Therefore, if you wish to convert Celsius to Fahrenheit, multiply the temperature given in Celsius degrees by 9/5 and add 32 degrees, as below.

Example: What is the Fahrenheit temperature equivalent to 20 degrees C?

$$F = \tfrac{9}{5}°C + 32$$

$$F = \tfrac{9}{5} \times 20 + 32 = 36 + 32 = 68 \text{ degrees F}$$

Convert these temperatures from Celsius to Fahrenheit:

°C	°F	°C	°F
30 degrees	_____	4 degrees	_____
23 degrees	_____	41 degrees	_____
18 degrees	_____	15 degrees	_____
27 degrees	_____	45 degrees	_____
8 degrees	_____		

Which of these might you expect to find in Death Valley in the summer? Which might you expect to find in Minnesota in January? Which might be a pleasant spring day in California?

Medicine and the Black Death

The Black Death first arrived in London in 1348, brought there by the fleas living on rats which came ashore from ships arriving from Asia. It was called the Black Death because of the way it appeared on the body. First, swellings appeared in the groin or armpits; then large black or purple splotches spread all over the body. When the patient died, the body became a black, smelly mess which revolted those left to bury it. The name of this terrible disease is *bubonic plague*, and it took only seven days to kill its victims. Only three of every ten people infected by it lived to tell the story.

For three centuries the population of London was periodically decimated by the Black Death. In 1348 about half the people living in London died from it, and the bill of mortality below illustrates the number of deaths from all causes and from the plague in one ten-month period in 1593. The figures on this chart are not completely accurate but are exact enough to get a good idea of just what the effect on the populace of London was in terms of cause of death.

In times of plague, all of those who could flee London did, thinking that the fresher air of the countryside would protect them from the plague's ravages. People thought that a poison in the air, which showed itself in bad smells, was the cause of the disease. All theaters (including the theaters where Shakespeare's plays were performed) and places where large groups of people gathered were closed until the disease had run its course, much as public places were closed in the United States during polio epidemics before the advent of the polio vaccine.

1593

Buried of all Difeafes, within London, and the Liberties thereof, From March to December 1593

Month	Date	Buried	Plague		Month	Date	Buried	Plague
March	17	230	3		August	4	1503	983
	24	251	31			11	1550	797
	31	219	29			18	1532	651
April	7	307	27			25	1508	449
	14	203	33		September	1	1490	507
	21	290	37			8	1210	563
	28	310	41			15	621	455
May	5	250	29			22	629	349
	12	339	38			29	450	330
	19	300	42		October	6	408	327
	26	450	58			13	422	323
June	2	410	62			20	330	308
	9	441	81			27	320	302
	16	399	99		November	3	310	301
	23	401	108			10	309	209
	30	850	118			17	301	107
July	7	1440	927			24	321	93
	14	1510	893		December	1	349	94
	21	1491	258			8	331	86
	28	1507	852			15	329	71
						22	386	39

The Total of all the Burials of the Time abovefaid: 25886
Whereof of the Plague: 11503

Medicine and the Black Death *(cont.)*

Various measures were taken by the city government to try to stop the plague. Houses in which someone was sick were considered to be infected, and the people living there were to be shut up within the house for a 28 day quarantine. Water pumps were required to be drained of ten buckets of water every evening after eight o'clock, with the water left to run into the streets. Infected houses and everything in them were to be aired in the 28 days they were quarantined, and none of the things belonging to the dead person were to be given away or sold. Understandably, these attempts to prevent or stop the plague created even greater hardships for the survivors, so sometimes they tried to hide the death of a family member and sneak his body out at night rather than allow officials to know about the death.

Thomas Cogan, an Englishman of that time, gave some advice about how to avoid catching the plague. He suggested that when leaving home, one should carry in his mouth a clove or two, a piece of cinnamon, orange peel, or a piece of angelica root and in the hand an orange, mint, or a sponge drenched in vinegar. He also provided the following recipe for a sweet-smelling elixir to be taken each morning before leaving home:

> ❖ 3 drams each Aloe Epaticum or Cicotrine, fine cinnamon and myrrh
>
> ❖ 1 ½ dram each Cloves, Mace, Lignum Aloe, Mastic, Bole Armeniac
>
> ❖ Mix all these things together in a clean mortar and take two penny-weights of the mixture in a half glass white wine. And so may you go safely into all infection of the air and plague.

In Elizabethan times there was no science of medicine as we think of it today, and people did not live as long. Most people died by the age of 50, and half the babies born were dead before their first birthdays. Almost nothing was known about hygiene, infection, or disease, and treatment for any illness remained about the same as it had been during the Middle Ages. Some doctors wore leather suits with a "breathing beak" of herbs and spices thought to prevent infection.

A standard treatment for almost any complaint was to "bleed" the patient. Doctors thought that illnesses were caused by bad blood, so the logical thing to do was to remove the bad blood with instruments meant for that purpose or by the use of leeches, sucking worms which would be attached to the patient's body. Of course, bleeding a person who had a high fever would be disastrous for the patient, for it would be removing the very fluid he needed to sustain life as well as injecting additional foreign organisms into his body.

Can the Plague Strike Again?

The plague hit Shakespeare's London many times, and when it did, a flood of people left the city to go to somewhere in the country where few people lived. All amusements which attracted many people shut down until the danger passed, and these included the theaters. Even though the part played by bacteria and viruses in causing disease had not yet been found, Londoners correctly connected close physical quarters with an increased chance of catching a devastating illness such as the Black Death.

During the 1930s, 1940s, and early 1950s, people in the United States reacted in a similar way to the dread disease of infantile paraysis, commonly known as polio, a disease which killed or crippled many children and adults. Outbreaks of polio always seemed to occur during the hot months of summer and to be spread when people were in crowded places. So in the cities, public places such as theaters, public swimming pools, and dancehalls shut down until the epidemic had run its course.

By the 1970s, however, scientists and those in the medical profession were sure that illnesses such as various forms of the plague, tuberculosis, polio, and venereal diseases had been conquered due to the polio vaccine and the many new forms of antibiotics, such as penicillin, which had been discovered. Recently, some scientists are beginning to rethink their beliefs about this, because some of the old diseases are again rearing their heads, and some new diseases have surfaced. An example of an old disease which seems to be making a comeback is *pneumonic plague*.

Pneumonic plague originates in humans from a bite by an infected flea carried by infected rats, but this terrible disease which affects the lungs and causes a quick death, can also be spread by the sputum expelled in the cough of an infected person. In fact, even though it can be treated with antibiotics such as tetracycline, it spreads so quickly its victims can die before their illness is diagnosed.

Pneumonic plague struck the country of India regularly before the advent of antibotics. At the turn of the century, this disease claimed the lives of ten million people. As late as 1947, 78,000 people died in India alone from it, but after antibiotics were used to treat the disease, it seemed to have died out. Now after not having appeared for 25 years, pneumonic plague has returned. By the end of the summer of 1994, 53 victims had already died from it in India. Tuberculosis is another of the old diseases which has developed into newer and more dangerous forms.

New diseases have also arisen, one of them being Lyme disease, which is caused by a bacterium which lives in deer ticks. As more and more people move into new homes built near wooded areas, and as they vacation in wooded areas, this disease continues to spread. Other new diseases include HIV and the hantavirus, both of which cause painful deaths.

Medicine and the Black Death Questions

Read the information on pages 108–110 relating to the Black Death. Read the questions below. Write your opinions and then discuss your answers with your classmates.

1. Have you ever seen any of the ingredients in the recipe?

    _____

    _____

2. If you wanted to get these ingredients, where would you go?

    _____

    _____

3. Why do you think people might have thought bad smells in the air caused the plague?

    _____

    _____

4. Might there have been a relationship between bad smells and infection?

    _____

    _____

5. What might lead to the belief that a person would have enough power to cause illness simply by wishing it as a witch would do?

    _____

    _____

6. Why do you think the plague never again occurred in London after the great fire?

    _____

    _____

An Exciting Time in Which to Live

Shakespeare lived during a time in which many things were happening. Sometimes this period is called the *Renaissance*, meaning "rebirth" or "revival." Below are some of the scientific and other events which happened between 1594 and 1616, the years in which Shakespeare wrote his plays.

❖ Tomatoes were introduced into England, and the first toilets were invented and installed at the queen's palace in Richmond. (1596)

❖ The first field hospitals and field dispensaries were developed. (1597)

❖ Dutch opticians invented the first telescope. (1600)

❖ Galileo investigated the laws of gravitation and oscillation. (1602)

❖ Johann Kepler reported on his findings about optics. (1604)

❖ The first study of modern anatomy was published. (1605)

❖ The first public library was established in Rome. (1605)

❖ Galileo invented the proportional compass. (1606)

❖ The colony of Jamestown was founded in Virginia. (1607)

❖ Galileo constructed the first astronomical telescope. (1608)

❖ Tea was shipped for the first time from China to Europe. (1609)

❖ Galileo discovered the moons on Jupiter. (1610)

❖ Simon Marius discovered the Andromeda Nebula. (1612)

❖ Copper coins were first used. (1613)

❖ Pocahontas married John Rolfe. (1614)

❖ Santorio Santorio published the first paper on metabolism and perspiration. (1614)

❖ Galileo was taken before the Inquisition for the first time, within a year after Shakespeare's death. The men of the Church were angry because he supported the Copernican theory that the earth revolved around the sun. He felt this was consistent with church doctrine and Biblical interpretation. The churchmen, however, ordered him not to hold or defend this theory. (1616)

Investigating Reflections

As revealed in the table of events on page 112, the last 16 years of Shakespeare's life saw a remarkable series of discoveries and inventions in the infant science of optics. These developments chiefly dealt with the manipulation of light rays by refraction and reflection. Experimenting with light rays can help us understand a number of things about optics today.

Reflections occur when rays of light hit a surface and bounce off again. Usually the best reflections are produced off shiny surfaces. Try one or more of these experiments to learn more about reflecting light. For these experiments you will need the following:

❖ three small mirrors
❖ piece of cardboard or playing card
❖ paper

❖ pen or pencil
❖ sticky tape
❖ small pieces of colored paper

1. **Change reflected light rays.** Cut a one–inch (2.5 cm) diameter hole in a piece of cardboard. Tape a comb across the hole. In a darkened room, stand the cardboard up on edge in front of a flashlight, so the light shines through the teeth of the comb. Hold a mirror in the lightbeams which come in through the teeth of the comb. Move the mirror in different directions. Observe what happens when you move the mirror.

2. **Write a secret message.** Put a piece of paper in front of a mirror. Looking in the mirror, carefully write a message by using the reflection to guide you. You will have written your message backwards.

3. **Make a kaleidoscope.** Tape three pocket mirrors together in a triangle with the reflecting surfaces inside. Taped together, the mirrors should now resemble a small pup tent. Stand the "pup tent" upright on a piece of cardboard and draw a line around the open triangle formed by the mirrors. Cut out the triangle of cardboard and tape it over the open end of the mirrors. Now drop the bits of colored paper inside. Cut out another triangle to tape over the other end. Punch a small hole in the center of this end and look inside the kaleidoscope. How many patterns can you see? What happens when you shake the kaleidoscope?

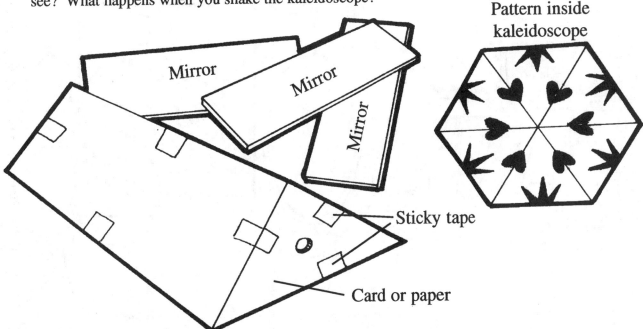

Pattern inside kaleidoscope

Mirror

Mirror

Mirror

Sticky tape

Card or paper

How Does a Telescope Work?

When the first telescopes were invented during Shakespeare's lifetime, it was a considerable achievement. Scientists were just beginning to understand how light travels through space. They learned how to magnify an image and bend its light before it reached the eye. They did this with the use of specially ground lenses.

To understand how a magnifying lens works, take a card or piece of cardboard you used in the activity on reflections. You will also need a comb, flashlight, sticky tape, a sheet of white paper, and a magnifying glass. Tape the comb over the hole in the card. Direct the light through the hole to shine across the piece of paper. Now put the magnifying glass in front of the comb, so that it acts as a lens. What happens to the light coming through the hole onto the paper? What is the difference between using and not using the magnifying glass?

This is because the magnifying glass is a convex lens. It focuses the light by bending it and causing it to come together.

Repeat the experiment, this time using a lens from the eyeglasses of a nearsighted person. How does the light behave now? This is because the eyeglass is a concave lens which spreads out the light instead of focusing it. When you understand this principle, you can make your own telescope.

Make your own telescope.

You will need a shaving mirror with a magnifying side, a small flat mirror, and a magnifying glass.

Stand the shaving mirror next to a window so the magnification side points toward the moon and stars. Hold the flat mirror in a spot where you can see the reflection of the shaving mirror in the middle. Now look at the reflection in the flat mirror through the magnifying glass. How do the moon and stars look now?

Although elementary telescopes were invented during Shakespeare's time, a reflecting telescope like this was not invented until Isaac Newton made one about 30 years after Shakespeare's death.

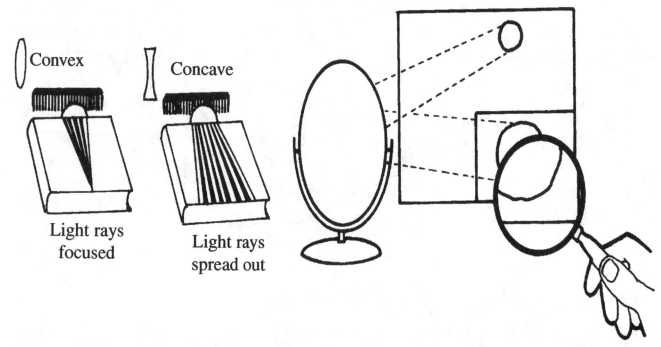

Convex

Concave

Light rays focused

Light rays spread out

Elizabeth I, the Queen

Princess Elizabeth of England was the older half-sister of Edward VI, but she was third in line to the throne when their father, King Henry VIII, died, so she remained a princess for eleven more years. When she finally did become queen, however, she ruled for 44 years, a time which has ever since been called the Elizabethan Age.

Queen Elizabeth I came to the throne in 1558 after many chaotic years for the British monarchy and for the people. When King Henry VIII died in 1547, the young Prince of Wales, Edward VI (only son of Henry and his third wife, Jane Seymour) succeeded him to the throne. Edward's reign was short, and he died at the age of 16. Young Lady Jane Grey, a cousin to the boy king, was proclaimed queen by ambitious members of the court; but nine days later she was deposed and banished to the Tower of London when Mary Tudor (oldest daughter of Henry and his first wife, Catherine of Aragon) claimed the throne.

Queen Mary, a Catholic, was very unpopular and called "Bloody Mary" by her subjects. She began her reign by re-establishing the Roman Catholic Church as the one and only church recognized in England. She had Lady Jane Grey beheaded, and then began a five-year persecution of the Protestant members of the Anglican Church her father had established in 1531. Thousands were tortured and killed in the name of religion. Mary also had her younger half-sister, Princess Elizabeth (the daughter of Henry and his second wife, Anne Boleyn) sent to the Tower. By the time Mary died in 1558, the English people were more than ready for a change, and they saw in Princess Elizabeth—who had been imprisoned by Mary as so many of their fellow citizens had—a chance for a fresh start.

It is said that when Elizabeth first entered London as queen she was received with great joy. The new queen, on her part, returned her love to the people. She never married, and when questioned about her not being able to produce an heir, she would reply that she was married to England and would hold up her hand to show the coronation ring on her finger.

On taking the throne, Elizabeth immediately proclaimed the official church to be the Church of England established by her father, and it seemed that things could return to normal. Times were bad, however. The English people were exhausted after years of religious turmoil under Mary. The army and navy were demoralized, food and goods were very expensive, and England had powerful enemies in France, Spain, and Scotland. However, Queen Elizabeth was up to the challenge, and the last years of her reign were relatively peaceful.

Elizabeth I, the Queen *(cont.)*

Queen Elizabeth loved music, dancing, and plays, and even sometimes composed music of her own. If she had not loved the arts, we probably would never have known of the works of William Shakespeare because a very powerful religious group, the Puritans, considered the theater "sinful, heathenish, lewd, and ungodly," attracting all the wrong sorts of people. They tried very hard to do away with anything having to do with it. Elizabeth placed Shakespeare's company under her protection, and they were known for the rest of her reign as "the Lord Chamberlain's Men." Several times a year the troupe would perform for the queen, and wherever they went in England, they were able to claim high prestige through the name of their royal patron.

The years Elizabeth reigned were ones of rebirth and growth for England. The arts flourished, especially the theater, poetry, and architecture. World-renowned schools were established, including Harrow, Jesus College at Oxford, Sidney Sussex and Corpus Christi Colleges at Cambridge, and Trinity College in Dublin, founded by Elizabeth, herself. Sir Francis Bacon published his *Essays, Civil and Moral*, and John Foxe published the first English edition of his *Book of Martyrs*. Sir Francis Drake saw the Pacific Ocean for the first time, and Sir Walter Raleigh discovered Virginia in the New World, claiming it for England and naming it after his Virgin Queen. The first machine to knit stockings was invented by William Lee of Cambridge, and heels first appeared on shoes. Tomatoes and tobacco were introduced into England, and the first toilets were installed in the Queen's Palace in Richmond. England had begun its endeavor to civilize and colonize the entire non-English world. It was a time unlike any other, before or since.

Activity

Elizabethan England had one of the world's greatest navies. Below is one of Her Majesty's ships which sailed around the world. One day it would be said that the sun never set on the British Empire. Next to the ship, list all the places you can find which were once claimed by England.

116

Making Comparisons

Use the chart below to compare the ways people lived during the Elizabethan Age and the ways most people you know live now. Remember, people lived in various ways then, just as we do now.

Situation	Elizabethan Age	Today
Housing		
Medical Treatment		
Educational Opportunities		
Food Available		
Religious Freedom		
Clothing for Men		
Clothing for Women		
Change from One Ruler/Leader to the Next		
Means to Travel		
Forms of Entertainment		
Opportunity to Get Ahead Socially		
Ships and Other Transportation		
Peace and Security		
Individual Rights		

Elizabethan Education

Most children and young people who lived during the time of Shakespeare did not go to school. Only the children of the well-to-do were afforded the privilege of an education because the common children had to help their parents make a living by working on the farm or in the shops. Some were apprenticed to tradesmen.

For the students who were able to go to school, the English Renaissance meant a "rebirth" of what was thought to be classical education. New finds of the ancient Greek and Roman civilizations had led those in charge of education to see Greek and Roman art and literature as ideal, so students were taught Greek and Latin, as well as French, which was the language spoken in the royal court. Almost everything was written in a way thought to parallel the classic. For example, most known Greek and Roman literature had been written in poetry; therefore, an educated person had to be able to write poetry, such as the sonnets on pages 132–134, and students were expected to memorize long passages from Greek and Latin poetry.

With few exceptions—such as the poor boys who were sponsored at Eton College each year—schools were for the wealthy and privileged sons of the nobility and the gentry, and parents paid fees to the schools so the students could attend. Rules in school were very strict, and schoolmasters, as teachers were then called, were expected to impose learning on their young charges with the help of regular whacks of a cane or birch whip. Only one of every 20 boys was deemed bright enough to go to school.

A student would not be sent to the office or merely scolded or ignored for being late; he would be hit hard on the hands or another part of his body. He would be similarly punished for not learning his lessons, turning in a paper which was not neat enough to please the schoolmaster, or accidentally dripping a spot of ink on the paper. No student would have thought of talking back to a schoolmaster, for he would have been expelled from the school, causing terrible shame for him and his family. No parent would have considered taking this power away from the schoolmaster, because it was believed that was the only way children could learn.

Most students lived at their schools as boarders, so the schoolmaster wielded a great deal of power over the students, including whether or not they got their meals. Meals were eaten at school, and the food was plain when compared to our tastes. Students went to school at six a.m., said prayers, and then went to breakfast. They worked on their studies until dinner at noon, and after dinner they worked again until supper at five, when they sang a hymn and attended a short religious service.

Students were expected to learn to read, write, and speak Latin. Girls were not allowed to become doctors, clergymen, or lawyers, so it was thought there was no point in educating girls. At least one hour each day was spent learning Bible scriptures and the catechism, and students were often expected to write a summary in Latin of the sermon preached that day.

Elizabethan Education *(cont.)*

The picture below shows a page from an Elizabethan reading book and the letters which were repeatedly copied until they were perfect. Pencils were not invented until the eighteenth century. All writing was painstakingly done with a quill pen and ink, which took a lot of time, and mistakes could not be easily corrected by erasing the mistake.

Quill pens were made of the feathers of geese, swans, or crows. The stem of a feather is hollow, so the inside of the quill could hold a little ink. This stem was split and carved to a point, so when the point was scratched against the paper, vellum, or parchment, it would leave ink, and you would have writing. It was a very tedious way to write, and mistakes were easy to make.

We do not use quill pens today because our more modern ballpoints and felt-tipped pens are so inexpensive and convenient. However, for fun, you might try copying the letters below using a quill pen you have made or an ink pen and ink from a stationery store, or use ink you have made yourself from berry juice.

A Methode

ſ	b	p	d	t
Sheares.	A Ball.	A Peare.	A Drum.	A Trumpet.
g	ʒ	v	♃	2
A Graſhopper.	A Jerkin.	A Vane.	The Sunne.	Zacheus.
k	ℭ	f	℔	s
A Key.	A Chaine.	A Filbert.	A Thimble.	A-Squirrell.

Crime and Punishment

Every historical period has had its share of people who break the law and are punished for it, and the Elizabethan Age is no exception. Even though the penalties for such activities as stealing, murdering, or committing treason were much more severe than they are today, some people continued to commit crimes, nonetheless. Moreover, some actions we now do not consider to be crimes were punishable. And, as with many other aspects of Elizabethan life, how you were treated if you were accused of a crime depended on whether you were poor or rich, a commoner or a noble.

One of the most common crimes committed in London was "cutpursing." There was no paper money then, pockets were not yet sewn into clothing, and coins were carried in purses which hung from the belt. A thief might take a person's money by cutting open the purse or by putting his hand into it. Usually, places at which your purse might be cut were public gatherings, such as plays, markets, or fairs. Church services were the most common places for cutpursing to happen because everyone was required to attend church.

"Hooking" was another common crime which happened often because there were no glass windows. A hooker would walk around carrying a wooden staff five or six feet (2 m) long in which a little hole had been bored at one end. A small hook was placed into this hole, and the hooker would use this device to reach inside open windows to retrieve clothing or purses when people were sleeping inside or when the rooms were unoccupied.

Dishonest horse dealers and gamblers were common. Horse dealers would use many means of making a horse look temporarily lively, such as pouring garlic juice into its nostrils, causing it to keep its head up until after the unwary buyer had given his money. And the prudent person did not travel through the countryside alone because highwaymen who stopped travelers and stole their goods and money could be in every wood and along any road.

Today most of us do not believe in witchcraft, but for some reason, beginning about 1560, many people had a great fear of witches. Witches were thought to be friends of the Devil, doing his dirty work. It was thought they were the causes of many illnesses, problems, and deaths which we now know to have been caused by natural conditions. Laws were passed against witchcraft, and the penalties for being convicted were severe. Just "practicing the evil art," whatever that meant, was cause for a year in prison. "Causing" a death by witchcraft would get the witch hanged or burned to death. Most people accused and convicted of witchcraft were probably what we know today to be mentally disturbed, or simply in the wrong place at the wrong time; but before the belief finally died out, many hundreds were killed. Shakespeare sometimes referred to witchcraft in his plays.

Crime and Punishment *(cont.)*

There were no police forces as we know them during Elizabethan times, and most people accused of crimes were apprehended by the magistrate or bailiff of a town or by the hue and cry. Punishments ranged from public humiliation to hanging or beheading, depending on the crime. A person found wandering the streets drunk would probably have to spend a day sitting in the stocks, such as in the drawing below. A merchant caught cheating a customer might be put into the stocks or the pillory (shown below). More serious crimes would have been punished by a public whipping or branding the face with a hot iron. Crimes of murder, highway robbery, and burglary were considered felonies and were punishable by hanging. Stealing anything worth more than a shilling was a felony.

The most serious crime of all was high treason, plotting to kill or overthrow the Queen. The punishment for high treason was by hanging and drawing and quartering. The traitor was hanged, taken down before he was dead, dragged face downward through the streets by a horse's tail, and then hacked into four pieces which were displayed in a public place as a warning to others who might be tempted to do what the traitor had done.

Noblemen were never hanged. They were beheaded with an axe, still a terrible way to go, but quicker than hanging, drawing, and quartering.

Most people put into prisons were put there for owing debts. The debtor would be put in prison until his debt had been paid. He was not provided food while he was in prison, and he was on his own to get someone to bring it to him. The prisoner who was rich, of course, suffered much less than the poor man, for he could have anything which he could pay for while he was in prison, except his freedom.

The Stocks

The Pillory

Activity: Today we call serious crimes *felonies* and less serious crimes *misdemeanors*. Ask a policeman, lawyer, or other person working in law enforcement for examples of each kind of crime and the punishment for it. Then compare what you learn about crime and punishment today with that in Elizabethan times.

Debate the Question

❖ *Will Severe and Public Punishment Prevent Crime?* ❖

A common question people sometimes discuss very heatedly today involves the use of severe punishment as a deterrent to crime.

Some say that if one knows there is a certain penalty for committing a certain crime and that the penalty will be painful or even lead to execution, then he will think twice before committing that crime, for the fear of the punishment will stop him. Occasionally, an advocate of severe penalties (particularly of capital punishment) will go so far as to say that punishments should be carried out in public or on television as a warning to everyone.

Those on the other side of the question say that most murders, for example, are committed in the "heat of passion" and that the person in a murderous rage will not stop to think whether or not he is going to be punished until after the act is over. The people who are against such severe penalties as capital punishment also point to the fact that the penalties end up never being applied fairly, so that criminals who have less mental ability than others or who belong to certain minority groups are punished more often than others.

In England during the Elizabethan Age, 226 crimes were punishable by hanging, including theft of more than one shilling in value, witchcraft, murder, and treason. All hangings were done in public. Knowing these facts, divide into teams of three or four to debate the following question:

Should persons convicted of murder receive the death penalty?

When planning the answer to the question with your team, please keep these points in mind:

1. Your team must come to an agreement as to the side you take in the debate.

2. You must research the question to come to an informed decision and base your opinion on facts, rather than just coming up with the answer you "feel" is correct.

3. You must respect opinions of others who disagree with you, just as you want others to respect your opinions.

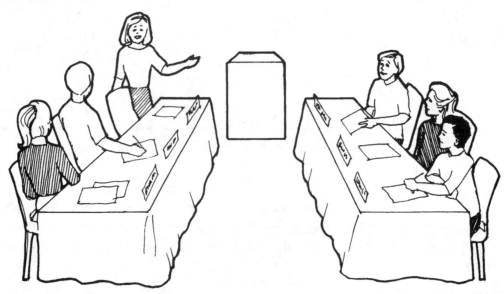

The Great Ships

The great ships of Queen Elizabeth's time were beautiful vessels, and the memory of them leads to many a romantic picture of billowing sails and peaceful waters. During the fifteenth century, the countries of Europe developed ships that could sail across the oceans, and they began to explore the world. Portugal, wanting to reach the "Spice Islands" in the East Indies, was one of the first to begin this great exploration. Most spices were not grown in Europe, so people would pay high prices for them. Soon the Portuguese were bringing home gold and silks, as well as spices, and other countries soon joined in the rush to get rich fast.

Spain wanted to do as Portugal did and sail the seven seas. By then people were beginning to realize that the earth was round, not flat as had been thought for centuries. Christopher Columbus persuaded the King and Queen of Spain to give him three ships, and he found what he believed to be the East Indies, but which later turned out to be islands off North America. The English started out far behind the Portuguese and Spanish, but during the reign of Queen Elizabeth, this changed as English ships went farther and farther afield until they, too, were sailing around the world. The race for the New World was on.

Much of the round-the-world sailing involved piracy, and nearly everyone living near the sea in England made money as a result. Merchants sold supplies to pirates and in turn were able to buy captured goods for low prices, later selling those goods for high profits. Of course, the pirates first kept whatever they wanted of the goods they stole. At sea, the pirates were evil, torturing and killing sailors and stealing from any ship they could find, but on shore they were merry souls and spent much time feasting, drinking, and partying.

Eventually, piracy made enemies of other countries for England. Many foreigners complained about the English pirates, and piracy threatened to lose for England the few friends it had. Because of this, Queen Elizabeth finally ordered her officials in the seaside countries to do everything they could to put down the pirates, and many were hanged. In the end, the government sent ships to round up pirate ships at sea, and most pirates either were caught and punished or changed their wicked ways.

At the same time that English piracy was being squelched, however, the seven seas began to witness a new evil: the slave trade. Many Spanish settlers in the West Indies had tried to enslave the local Indians to grow sugar cane, a very profitable crop. The Indians were not physically able to do the work, however, and many of them died. The landowners wanted to make slaves of the much stronger Africans, instead. Because the government of Spain outlawed trade with anyone except other Spanish, and at the same time placed very high taxes on slaves, many Spanish landowners were willing to break the law and trade with non-Spanish slave traders. The French and English soon realized they could made a lot of money selling slaves in the Spanish colonies. This terrible use of beautiful ships for a most ugly purpose continued for many years, until slavery was finally abolished in all of North America.

The Great Ships *(cont.)*

Some English seamen became famous for their exploits. Sir Francis Drake, for example, began by attacking Spanish ships and then decided to capture Spanish treasure while it was still on the mainland rather than at sea. He was able to amass a considerable fortune with his small fleet of ships and was later knighted by the Queen. Other famous sea captains of the time included John Oxenham and John Hawkins.

The highlight of the period for England was the English defeat of the Spanish Armada in 1588. The Spanish king wanted to conquer England. Under Elizabeth, England was a Protestant country, and the king wanted to restore it to the Catholic faith. The English knew the Spanish were intending to launch an assault on them but did not know when. The most important ships in the English fleet were the ones that belonged to the Queen, but there were not enough of them, so the government asked all the seaside towns to send armed merchant ships. Not all the towns complied with the request, but many did. London alone sent thirty ships.

The Armada arrived near Plymouth on July 29 and began sailing up the coast. The English fleet was able to position itself outside the Spanish fleet, following along closely. Once inside the English Channel, two things happened which hurt the Spanish dearly. One of their largest ships blew up. Another, the *Rosario*, broke its foremast, so she could not keep up with the rest of the fleet. Finally, the English attacked on August 8, near Gravelines on the coast of France. Soon the Armada was out of ammunition and had many ships damaged, whereupon they set sail to return to Spain.

Few things built by man can equal the wonderful sailing ships of the fifteenth century for grace and beauty. They have inspired poetry and wonderful works of art. And even though they were used for some terrible purposes, such as piracy and the slave trade, the ships continue to evoke awe and wonder in a way which few of our modern craft can do. The picture on page 125 shows a cross-section of a typical ship in Elizabethan times. Using the accompanying index, locate and identify by number the following items, afterward using the dictionary to determine the purpose of each:

- ❖ mainmast _____ _____
- ❖ keel _____ _____
- ❖ forecastle (fo'c's'le) _____ _____
- ❖ foremast _____ _____
- ❖ bowsprit _____ _____
- ❖ captain's cabin _____ _____
- ❖ poop-deck _____ _____
- ❖ main cabin _____ _____
- ❖ gallery _____ _____
- ❖ main gun _____ _____
- ❖ brig _____ _____
- ❖ main hatch _____ _____

Writing: Imagine that you are cabin boy on this ship. What cargo does your ship carry? Where does it sail? What are your duties? Write a log, or diary, of the time you spend on board.

The Great Ships *(cont.)*

1. mainmast 2. foremast 3. mizzen 4.bonaventure 5.bowsprit 6.gallery 7. poop deck 8.quarterdeck 9. forecastle 10. main gun 11. capstan 12. helmsman using whipstaff connected to rudder tiller 13. captain's cabin 14. main cabin—for officers and gentlemen 15. brig 16. lamp room 17. main hatch 18. galley stove 19. ships stores (i.e., sails, ropes, etc.) 20. ships stores (food, water, wine, etc.) 21. ballast—to help the ship's stability 22. keel 23. small deck car- ronade 24. "beak"

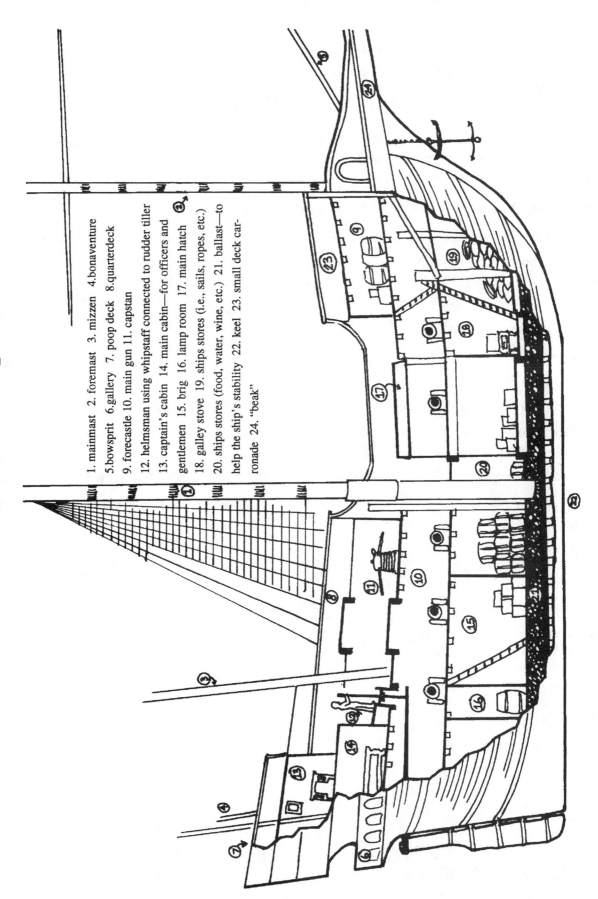

Build a Model Pageant

Today we think of a pageant as being an elaborate public display such as you might see at halftime during a major football game or as scenes set up and acted out during the holidays. For centuries, though, a pageant was the name for a movable stage.

The morality plays popular in medieval times and still being produced during Shakespeare's day were presented on pageants such as the one below. These would be pulled through the town from one pre-arranged place to another. The members of the audience could either follow one pageant around (thereby seeing one part of the play more than once) or they could stand in one place, knowing that in time all parts of the play would pass by them so they would see everything.

To make a model pageant you will need the following:

❖ the bottom of a cardboard box such as a shoe box

❖ plain paper for covering box

❖ pieces of heavy cardboard or balsa wood for the wheels

❖ brass paper fasteners

❖ craft sticks

❖ a piece of wire for the tongue

❖ pieces of fabric or colored paper for scenery

❖ scissors and glue

Directions:

1. Turn the box upside down and cover with paper.

2. Cut heavy cardboard or balsa into four wheels and attach to box with brass fasteners.

3. Poke two small holes into end of the box and bend and insert wire as shown to form a tongue for pulling the pageant.

4. Cut slits in one side of the top of the box and insert craft sticks to hold up background scenery.

5. Design and make scenery for play on top of the box much as you would for a diorama inside a box.

6. If you wish, make stick people to represent the actors in the play.

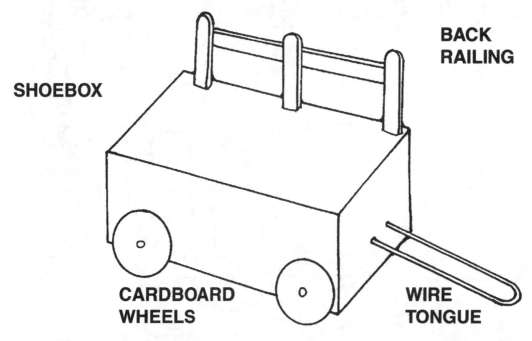

BACK RAILING

SHOEBOX

CARDBOARD WHEELS

WIRE TONGUE

Improving the Air with Sachets

Elizabethans thought that bad smells caused illness, and they had many suggestions as to how to prevent or cover up odors. There were no sanitary facilities such as we have: no bathroom facilities, sewers, or waste treatment plants. People, (even the rich), seldom took baths, and garbage was thrown into the streets. The role of bacteria in causing illness had not yet been discovered, so while they correctly associated bad smells with illness and decay, they thought the smells were a cause of disease rather than a result of the bacteria which did cause it. Can you imagine how a city like London, full of people dumping their waste materials anywhere, must have smelled?

Herbs and plants were used in various ways to cover up smells, and many are still used because, although we use sanitary measures to control our environment, we still like their pleasant smells. Some favorites of the Elizabethans included:

❖ pennyroyal
❖ marjoram
❖ pot marjoram
❖ rosemary

❖ wintergreen
❖ violet
❖ yarrow
❖ clary sage

❖ damask and provence roses
❖ geranium
❖ lavender
❖ lemon verbena

People today still grow these plants for their beauty and their fragrance. One way of capturing the delightful aroma of herbs is by using them in sachets, small packets of sweet-smelling herbs which can be placed under a pillow, or tucked in among linens or clothing in drawers and closets. Sachets are easy to make. You will need the following:

❖ a package of potpourri available at drugstores or other shops
❖ small pieces fabric (Satins and laces are especially nice.)
❖ needle and thread
❖ scissors

Cut fabric or lace into the shape of your choice. Cut two pieces for each sachet. Many people like to use heart shapes, but any shape is fine. Stitch the matching pieces together at the edges, leaving a small open area for stuffing. Stuff potpourri in through the opening, and then sew the opening shut. Trim and decorate with laces, ribbons, and small flowers. You now have a sweet-smelling sachet to give as a gift or to scent your clothing.

Elizabethan Half-masques

Queen Elizabeth I and many wealthy people of her time enjoyed having and going to parties of all kinds, particularly when music and dancing were part of the entertainment. Masqued balls, such as the one at which Romeo met Juliet, were popular, and half-masques added a little spice to the fun.

You can make a half-masque for yourself from papier-mâché. This is what you need:

❖ flat-bottomed dish or tray about 6 inches (15 cm) across (approximately the width of your face)

❖ strips of newspaper of paper towels

❖ wallpaper paste

❖ objects such as paperclips, spools, or egg carton cups suitable for forming features

❖ pieces of cardboard

❖ tempera paint, markers

❖ craft stick

Directions:

The half-masque should be of a size to approximately fit the top half of your face, from the top of your head to just about the tip of your nose; so you need to get it as close to the size and shape of your face as possible. Adjust directions so the masque will fit.

1. Wet paper strips in wallpaper paste.

2. On the greased bottom of upturned dish or tray, apply two layers of paper strips.

3. Using any objects you need and pieces of cardboard, add features that are to stand out such as the nose. Mold the nose area up from underneath so the masque will fit to your face.

4. Glue a craft stick to the side of the masque to be used as a holder.

5. Cover everything except the stick with additional layers of papier- mâché. Let dry.

6. Remove the bowl or tray and then paint your masque.

Note: Popular shapes for half-masques were animals such as cats and lions. After the base coat of your paint is dry, use a small brush or markers to paint on eyelashes and expressions.

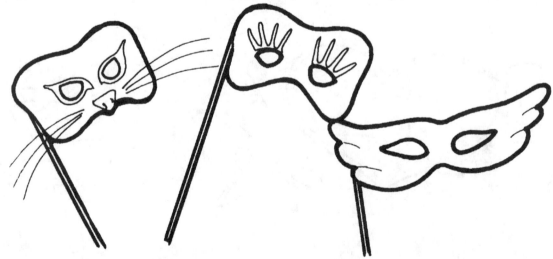

The Food of the People

Most people today are accustomed to having a wide variety of foods to eat. Because we have modern means of freezing and preserving large quantities of foods, and because we have huge grain elevators in which to store wheat, rice, and other cereal grains, we may go to a large supermarket and buy almost any food imaginable. In fact, new foods and new ways of producing and serving foods are developed every day, so on a trip to the grocery store, we may choose among thousands of different foods.

During the Elizabethan Age this was not so. Most of what the Elizabethans ate fell into categories of foods which most people raised for themselves: meats, such as beef, mutton, pork, veal, and kid, as well as chicken, goose, and fish; and a few vegetables, such as cabbages, onions, turnips, and potatoes. Bread was a staple food, and the grain with which to make it was grown by each family. Cheese was made from the milk of the family's cow or goat, and eggs would be had from their own chickens.

Relatively few foods were bought, although any spices or luxury items like sugar were increasingly imported from other lands in the East Indies or the Mediterranean. These included pepper, cinnamon, nutmeg, ginger, and cloves, and occasional fruits such as oranges, raisins, and prunes. The increased availability of sugar in the fifteenth and sixteenth centuries, due to trade made possible by the great ships, allowed those who could afford it to add preserves, marmalades, sweets, marzipan, and puddings to their diets. However, sugar remained expensive for many years.

Although rising and beginning work at daybreak, the typical adult ate only two meals per day—dinner at around eleven o'clock in the morning and supper at about five o'clock in the afternoon. Young children might have a light breakfast of bread and cheese, but an adult usually had to be satisfied with only two meals.

Try to find out which of the following foods were common or not common in England in the year 1500 and indicate with a check in the proper column.

Food	Common in 1500	Not Common in 1500
❖ tomatoes		
❖ bananas		
❖ canned tuna		
❖ cornflakes		
❖ honey		
❖ bacon		
❖ hamburgers		
❖ popcorn		
❖ ice cream		
❖ pizza		
❖ steak		
❖ hot dogs		
❖ French bread		
❖ orange juice		

Refrigerating Foods: a New Invention

Today most people take refrigerators for granted. It seems they have always been around for us to use, yet the process for refrigerating meats—thereby extending the time they would be kept without having to dry or salt them—was not developed until 1934.

The ability of ice to preserve food has been known since the seventeenth century, and in England there are still many "ice houses" left from the days wealthy Victorians could extend the length of time their meats would last before spoiling. The ice in these ice houses kept foods cold, because it takes heat to melt the ice. This heat was withdrawn from the stored foods, and as the heat was withdrawn, the temperature of the food went down, thereby giving it a longer storage time.

Refrigerators operate on a related principle. When liquids evaporate, they take heat from their surroundings. As shown in the drawing below, a liquid such as freon circulates through a system of tubes so that there is a constant cycle of evaporation and condensation. As the liquid in the tubes evaporates, it takes heat from the foods in the refrigerator.

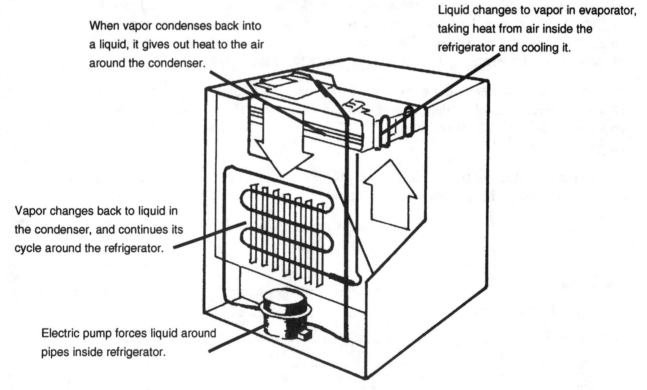

When vapor condenses back into a liquid, it gives out heat to the air around the condenser.

Liquid changes to vapor in evaporator, taking heat from air inside the refrigerator and cooling it.

Vapor changes back to liquid in the condenser, and continues its cycle around the refrigerator.

Electric pump forces liquid around pipes inside refrigerator.

Have you ever made homemade ice cream? An ice cream freezer utilizes the same principle as the refrigerator. In your classroom, use an ice cream freezer brought in by your teacher or a parent to make ice cream, following the instructions given with the freezer, and record the following:

❖ How long did it take to freeze the ice cream? _____

❖ What did you add to the ice to lower the temperature? _____

On the back of this paper, describe the principle of freezing ice cream as you have observed it.

Elizabethan Sonnets

During the Elizabethan Age an educated person was expected to write poetry and to be able to recite from memory the classical poems of Greece and Rome. A favorite type of poem written in English was the *sonnet*.

Shakespeare did not invent the sonnet; Petrarch, a fourteenth century poet did, but Shakespeare has been associated with it for a long time because of the 154 sonnets he wrote, considered some of the English-speaking world's most beautiful lines. When the term *Elizabethan sonnet* is used, it refers to sonnets constructed like those Shakespeare wrote. Most sonnets consisted of single, fourteen-line poems, but sometimes Elizabethan poets would write whole narratives in sonnet form.

Like many types of poetry, a sonnet generally follows a set of rules. The rules for the structure of an Elizabethan or Shakespearean sonnet are as follows:

1. There are 14 lines altogether.

    A. There are three sets of four lines, called *quatrains*

    B. There are two lines at the end called a *couplet*

2. Each line contains ten syllables with every other syllable accented, usually beginning with the second syllable on each line.

3. The sonnet has a formal rhyme scheme which is as follows:

    abab

    cdcd

    efef

    gg

In this rhyme scheme the "a's" rhyme with each other, the 'b's" rhyme with each other, and so forth.

4. The sonnet also has a *thematic structure.* Usually, the first two quatrains set up a problem, the third quatrain begins to answer the problem, and the ending couplet tries to solve the problem.

On the following page are two Shakespearean sonnets with the quatrains, couplets, and rhyme scheme identified for you on the first one. Can you identify the quatrains, couplets, and rhyme schemes of the second and third sonnets?

Challenge: What are the problems and solutions of these sonnets?

Elizabethan Sonnets *(cont.)*

116

Let me not to the marriage of true minds	*a*
Admit impediments. Love is not love	*b*
Which alters when it alteration finds,	*a*
Or bends with the remover to remove.	*b*
Oh no! It is an ever-fixed mark	*c*
That looks on tempests and is never shaken.	*d*
It is the star to every wandering bark,	*c*
Whose worth's unknown, although his height be taken.	*d*
Love's not Time's fool, though rosy lips and cheeks	*e*
Within his bending sickle's compass come.	*f*
Love alters not with his brief hours and weeks,	*e*
But bears it out even to the edge of doom.	*f*
If this be error and upon me proved,	*g*
I never writ, nor no man ever loved.	*g*

73

That time of year thou mayst in me behold
When yellow leaves, or none, or few, do hang
Upon those boughs which shake against the cold,
Bare ruined choirs where late the sweet birds sang.
In me thou see'st the twilight of such day
As after sunset fadeth in the west,
Which by and by black night doth take away,
Death's second self, that seals up all in rest.
In me thou see'st the glowing of such fire,
That on the ashes of his youth doth lie
As the deathbed whereon it must expire,
Consumed with that which it was nourished by.
This thou perceiv'st, which makes thy love more strong,
To love that well which thou must leave ere long.

choirs: part of a church

Elizabethan Sonnets *(cont.)*

106

When in the chronicle of wasted time
I see descriptions of the fairest wights,
And beauty making beautiful old rhyme
In praise of ladies dead and lovely knights,
Then, in the blazon of sweet beauty's best,
Of hand, of foot, of lip, of eye, of brow,
I see their antique pen would have expressed
Even such a beauty as you master now.
So all their praises are but prophesies
Of this our time, all you prefiguring,
And, for they looked but with divining eyes,
They had not skill enough your worth to sing.
For we, which now behold these present days,
Have eyes to wonder, but lack tongues to praise.

5

Those hours that with gentle work did frame
The lovely gaze where every eye doth dwell
Will play the tyrants to the very same
And that unfair which fairly doth excel.
For never-resting time leads summer on
To hideous winter and confounds him there,
Sap checked with frost and lusty leaves quite gone,
Beauty o'ersnowed and bareness everywhere.
Then, were not summer's distillation left,
A liquid prisoner pent in walls of glass,
Beauty's effect with beauty were bereft,
Nor it, nor no remembrance what it was.
But flowers distilled, though they with winter meet,
Leese but their show. Their substance still lives sweet.

wights: men; *blazon*: praise; *for*: except that; *divining*:
foreseeing; *leese*: lose

Elizabethan Sonnets *(cont.)*

17

Who will believe my verse in time to come
If it were filled with your most high deserts?
Though yet, Heaven knows, it is but as a tomb
Which hides your life and shows not half your parts.
If I could write the beauty of your eyes
And in fresh numbers number all your graces,
The age to come would say, "This poet lies,
Such heavenly touches ne'er touched earthly faces."
So should my papers, yellowed with their age,
Be scorned, like old men of less truth than tongue,
And your true rights be termed a poet's rage
And stretched meter of an antique song.
But were some child of yours alive that time,
You should live twice, in it and in my rhyme.

18

Shall I compare thee to a summer's day?
Thou art more lovely and more temperate.
Rough winds do shake the darling buds of May,
And summer's lease hath all too short a date.
Sometimes too hot the eye of Heaven shines,
And often is his gold complexion dimmed.
And every fair from fair sometime declines,
By chance or nature's changing course untrimmed.
But thy eternal summer shall not fade,
Nor lose possession of that fair thou owest,
Nor shall Death brag thou wander'st in his shade
When in eternal lines to time thou grow'st.
So long as men can breathe, or eyes can see,
So long lives this, and this gives life to thee.

parts: good qualities; *rage:* enthusiasm; *stretched:*
exaggerated; *eye of heaven:* the sun; *untrimmed:* shorn of
beauty

The News Ballad

Not everyone living in the Elizabethan Age read Greek and Latin and wrote sonnets. After all, only about one of every 20 boys went to school, and very few girls, but just as the common and uneducated people loved the theater and went to plays, so, too, did they like poetry, but of a different kind.

The most popular poetry was the *news ballad*. Hundreds of these ballads were written about almost any sensational event of the day, often exaggerated and made melodramatic as the newspaper tabloids are today. They were a sort of everyman's gossip poem about battles, royalty, scandalous crimes, grievances, marvelous events, and executions. They often were in the form of laments of a criminal for the wicked life he had led.

On any market day or public execution, or at any place where a large crowd was gathered, there would be a ballad singer, or minstrel, who sang his songs and sold them for a penny each. The following ballad written by Thomas Deloney and printed by Thomas Scarlet in 1591 is typical of the news ballad. Its story was based on the true one which had caused quite a scandal in Devon.

Ulalia was forced by her parents to marry a rich old man named Mr. Page, even though she wanted to marry George Strangwidge. Ulalia persuaded George Strangwidge and two accomplices to strangle Mr. Page in his bed. All four perpetrators of the crime were later hanged for it, but public sympathy went with the girl, because most people thought she should have been able to marry anyone she wanted to marry.

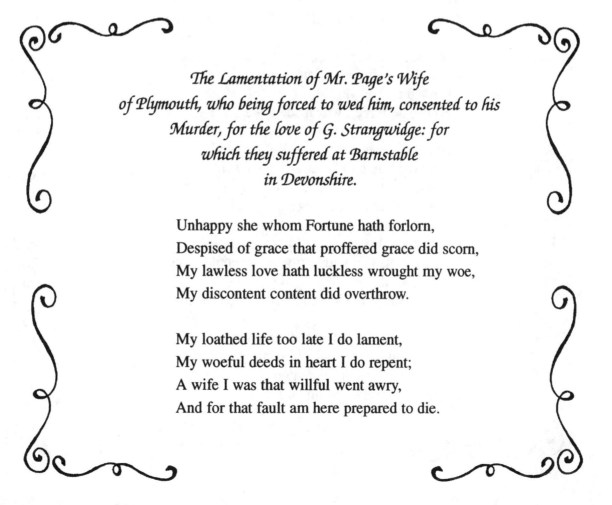

The Lamentation of Mr. Page's Wife
of Plymouth, who being forced to wed him, consented to his
Murder, for the love of G. Strangwidge: for
which they suffered at Barnstable
in Devonshire.

Unhappy she whom Fortune hath forlorn,
Despised of grace that proffered grace did scorn,
My lawless love hath luckless wrought my woe,
My discontent content did overthrow.

My loathed life too late I do lament,
My woeful deeds in heart I do repent;
A wife I was that willful went awry,
And for that fault am here prepared to die.

The News Ballad *(cont.)*

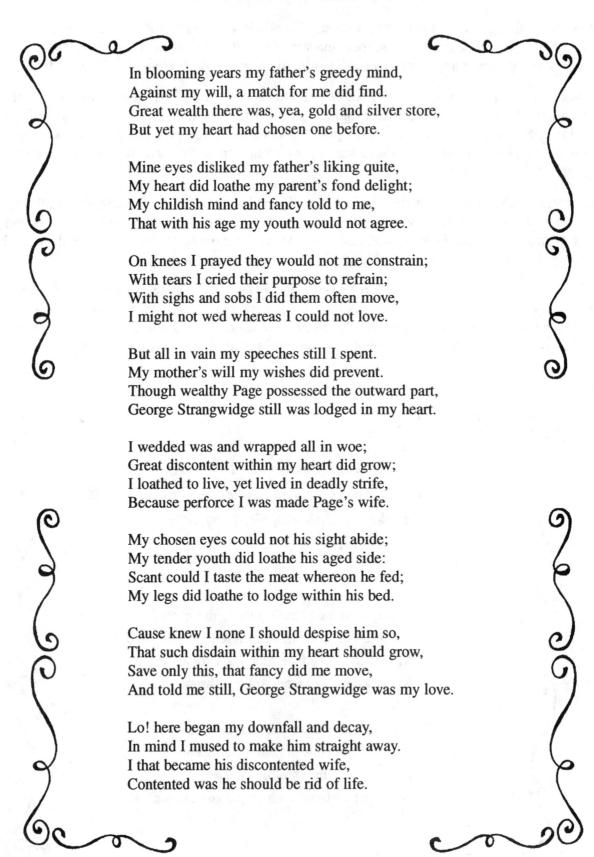

In blooming years my father's greedy mind,
Against my will, a match for me did find.
Great wealth there was, yea, gold and silver store,
But yet my heart had chosen one before.

Mine eyes disliked my father's liking quite,
My heart did loathe my parent's fond delight;
My childish mind and fancy told to me,
That with his age my youth would not agree.

On knees I prayed they would not me constrain;
With tears I cried their purpose to refrain;
With sighs and sobs I did them often move,
I might not wed whereas I could not love.

But all in vain my speeches still I spent.
My mother's will my wishes did prevent.
Though wealthy Page possessed the outward part,
George Strangwidge still was lodged in my heart.

I wedded was and wrapped all in woe;
Great discontent within my heart did grow;
I loathed to live, yet lived in deadly strife,
Because perforce I was made Page's wife.

My chosen eyes could not his sight abide;
My tender youth did loathe his aged side:
Scant could I taste the meat whereon he fed;
My legs did loathe to lodge within his bed.

Cause knew I none I should despise him so,
That such disdain within my heart should grow,
Save only this, that fancy did me move,
And told me still, George Strangwidge was my love.

Lo! here began my downfall and decay,
In mind I mused to make him straight away.
I that became his discontented wife,
Contented was he should be rid of life.

The News Ballad *(cont.)*

Methinks the heavens cry vengeance for my fact,
Methinks the world condemns my monstrous act,
Methinks within my conscience tells me true,
That for that deed hell-fire is my due.

My pensive soul doth sorrow for my sin,
For which offense my soul doth bleed within;
But mercy, Lord! for mercy still I cry:
Save thou my soul, and let my body die.

Well could I wish that Page enjoyed his life,
So that he had some other to his wife:
But never could I wish, of low or high,
S'longer life than see sweet Strangwidge die.

Oh woe is me! that had no greater grace
To stay till he had run out Nature's race.
My deeds I rue, but I do repent
That to the same my Strangwidge gave consent.

You parents fond, that greedy-minded be,
And seek to graft upon the golden tree,
Consider well and rightful judges be,
And give you doom twixt parent's love and me.

I was their child, and bound for to obey,
Yet not to love where I no love could lay.
I married was to muck and endless strife;
But faith before had made me Strangwidge' wife.

O wretched world, who cankered rust doth blind!
And cursed men who bear a greedy mind!
And hapless I, whom parents did force so,
To end my days in sorrow, shame, and woe.

You Denshire dames, and courteous Cornwall knights,
That here are come to visit woeful wights,
Regard my grief, and mark my woeful end,
But to your children be a better friend.

The News Ballad (cont.)

And thou, my dear, that for my fault must die,
Be not afraid the sting of death to cry.
Like as we lived and loved together true,
So both at once we'll bid the world adieu.

Ulalia, thy friend, doth take her last farewell,
Whose soul with thee in Heav'n shall ever dwell.
Sweet Saviour Christ, do thou my soul receive!
The world I do with all my heart forgive.

And parents now, whose greedy minds do show
Your heart's desire, and inward beauty woe,
Mourn you no more, for now my heart doth tell,
Ere day be done my soul shall be full well.

And Plymouth proud, I bid thee now farewell.
Take heed, you wives, let not your hands rebel.
And farewell, life, wherein such sorrow shows,
And Welcome, death, that doth my corpse enclose.

And now, sweet Lord, forgive me my misdeeds!
Repentance cries for soul that inward bleeds.
My soul and body I commend to thee,
That with thy blood from death redeemed me.

Lord! Bless our Queen with long and happy life,
And send true peace betwixt each man and wife;
And give all parents wisdom to foresee
The match is marred where minds do not agree.

138

Write a News Ballad of Your Own

The news ballad you have just read is really a tear-jerker, isn't it? In it, Ulalia cries about how horrible it was to be married to an old man, and she begs other parents not to give in to the greedy temptation of making their daughters marry for money lest they meet the same terrible fate which she has met. Does she seem repentant about killing Page? Or is she only sorry she has caused the death-by-hanging of herself and George Strangwidge? Do you feel the same pity for her that apparently her fellow townspeople felt when she was hanged?

For centuries ballads like this were written about people who had committed crimes, usually scandalous ones. In America during the 1800's, many were written about such people as Jesse James and Lizzy Borden, and in Medieval England they were written about Robin Hood. These ballads tended to romanticize people who had ignored or abused certain laws of their society and indicated that their crimes were justified. How do you feel about them? Could Ulalia's story have happened today?

Activity

Using any event which is newsworthy today, such as one you take from a newspaper or popular magazine, write a ballad of your own. The ballad has an easy and simple structure to follow. You need follow only these rules:

1. There are four lines to each stanza.

2. Each line contains ten syllables which generally are stressed on the even-numbered syllables of each line. You sometimes need to slur words together to make them fit.

3. This rhyme scheme is aabb—that is, the first two lines of a stanza rhyme with each other, and the third and fourth lines rhyme with each other. The lines of one stanza do not have to rhyme with the lines of another.

Have fun!

❖ ❖ ❖ ❖

_____   _____

_____   _____

_____   _____

_____   _____

_____   _____

_____   _____

_____   _____

Another Kind of Ballad

Besides the news ballad, of course, other types of ballads—like "Robin and Little John"—appeared in old England and were passed down by word of mouth. Robin Hood was a bandit who robbed the rich and gave to the poor in a day and age in England when a few people were very wealthy and most people were very poor. He lived about 200 years before Shakespeare wrote his plays and sonnets, but minstrels and storytellers were telling his story in Shakespeare's England, even as it is still told today in books, poems, movies, and songs.

Most of the stories and ballads, such as this one, romanticized Robin Hood and made him into a hero. Because most people lived in terrible poverty, and many resented the enormous taxes and rents they had to pay to rich landlords, it was easy for them to see Robin Hood and his men as almost bigger than life. Many stories about him told of certain feats in which he saved the life or the home of someone. Other stories were like the one in this ballad, telling of the camaraderie among his men and the merry times they had together in Sherwood Forest where they lived.

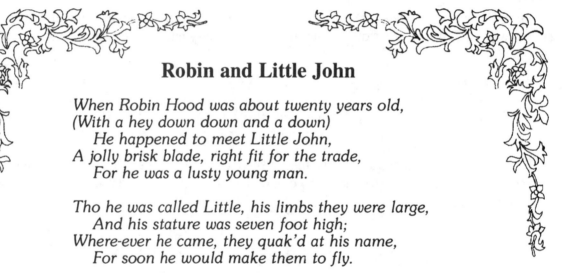

Robin and Little John

When Robin Hood was about twenty years old,
(With a hey down down and a down)
    He happened to meet Little John,
A jolly brisk blade, right fit for the trade,
    For he was a lusty young man.

Tho he was called Little, his limbs they were large,
    And his stature was seven foot high;
Where-ever he came, they quak'd at his name,
    For soon he would make them to fly.

How they came acquainted, I'll tell you in brief,
    If you will but listen a while;
For this very jest, amongst all the rest,
    I think it may cause you to smile.

Bold Robin Hood said to his jolly bowmen,
    "Pray tarry you here in this grove;
And see that you all observe well my call,
    While through the forest I rove.

"We have had no sport for these fourteen long days,
    Therefore now abroad will I go;
Now should I be beat, and cannot retreat,
    My horn I will presently blow."

Then did he shake hands with his merry men all,
    And bid them at present good b'w'ye;
Then as near a brook his journey he took,
    A stranger he chanced to espy.

Another Kind of Ballad *(cont.)*

Robin Hood and Little John *(cont.)*

They happened to meet on a long narrow bridge,
  And neither of them would give way;
Quoth bold Robin Hood, and sturdily stood,
  "I'll show you right Nottingham play."

With that from his quiver an arrow he drew,
  A broad arrow with a goose-wing;
The stranger reply'd, "I'll liquor thy hide,
  If thou offerst to touch the string."

Quoth bold Robin Hood, "Thou dost prate like an ass,
  For were I to bend but my bow,
I could send a dart quite thro thy proud heart,
  Before thou couldst strike me one blow."

"Thou talkst like a coward," the stranger reply'd;
  "Well armed with a long bow you stand,
To shoot at my breast, while I, I protest,
  Have nought but a staff in my hand."

"The name of a coward," quoth Robin, "I scorn,
  Wherefore my long bow I'll lay by;
And now, for thy sake, a staff will I take,
  The truth of thy manhood to try."

Then Robin step'd to a thicket of trees,
  And chose him a staff of ground-oak;
Now this being done, away he did run
  To the stranger, and merrily spoke:

"Lo! see my staff, it is lusty and tough,
  Now here on the bridge we will play;
Whoever falls in, the other shall win
  The battle, and so we'll away."

"With all my whole heart," the stranger reply'd;
  "I scorn in the least to give out;"
This said, they fell to 't without more dispute,
  And their staffs they did flourish about.

And first Robin he gave the stranger a bang,
  So hard that it made his bones ring;
The stranger he said, "This must be repaid,
  I'll give you as good as you bring.

Another Kind of Ballad (cont.)

Robin Hood and Little John (cont.)

"So long as I'm able to handle my staff,
    To die in your debt, friend, I scorn;"
Then to it each goes, and follow'd their blows,
    As if they had been threshing corn.

The stranger gave Robin a crack on the crown,
    Which caused the blood to appear;
Then Robin, enrag'd, more fiercely engag'd,
    And follow'd his blows more severe.

So thick and so fast did he lay it on him,
    With a passionate fury and ire,
At every stroke, he made him to smoke,
    As if he had been all on fire.

O then into fury the stranger he grew,
    And gave him a damnable look,
And with it a blow that laid him full low,
    And tumbl'd him into the brook.

"I prithee, good fellow, O where art thou now?"
    The stranger, in laughter, he cry'd;
Quoth bold Robin Hood, "Good faith, in the flood,
    And floating along with the tide.

"I needs must acknowledge thou art a brave soul;
    With thee I'll no longer contend;
For needs must I say, thou hast got the day,
    Our battle shall be at an end."

Then unto the bank he did presently wade,
    And pull'd himself out by a thorn;
Which done, at the last, he blowd a loud blast
    Straitway on his fine bugle-horn.

The echo of which through the vallies did fly,
    At which his stout bowmen appeared,
All cloth-ed in green, most gay to be seen;
    So up to their master they steer'd.

"O what's the matter?" quoth William Stutely;
    "Good master, you are wet to the skin";
"No matter," quoth he; "the lad which you see,
    In fighting, hath tumbl'd me in."

Another Kind of Ballad *(cont.)*

Robin Hood and Little John *(cont.)*

"He shall not go scot-free," the others reply'd;
    So strait they were seizing him there,
To duck him likewise; but Robin Hood cried,
    "He is a stout fellow, forbear.

"There's no one shall wrong thee, friend, be not afraid;
    These bowmen upon me do wait;
There's threescore and nine; if thou wilt be mine,
    Thou shalt have my livery strait,

"And other accoutrements fit for a man.
    Speak up, jolly blade, never fear;
I'll teach you also the use for the bow,
    To shoot at the fat fallow-deer."

"O here is my hand," the stranger reply'd,
    "I'll serve you with all my whole heart;
My name is John Little, a man of good mettle;
    Ne'er doubt me, for I'll play my part."

"His name shall be alter'd," quoth William Stutely,
    "And I will his godfather be;
Prepare then a feast, and none of the least,
    For we will be merry," quoth he.

They presently fetched in a brace of fat does,
    With humming strong liquor likewise;
They lov'd what was good; so, in the greenwood,
    This pretty sweet babe they baptize.

He was, I must tell you but seven foot high,
    And, may be, an ell in the waste;
A pretty sweet lad; much feasting they had;
    Bold Robin the christening grac'd.

With all his bowmen, which stood in a ring,
    And were of the Nottingham breed;
Brave Stutely comes then, with seven yoemen,
    And did in this manner proceed.

"This infant was called John Little," quoth he,
    Which name shall be changed anon;
The words we'll transpose, so wherever he goes,
    His name shall be called Little John."

Another Kind of Ballad *(cont.)*

Robin Hood and Little John *(cont.)*

They all with a shout made the elements ring,
  So soon as the office was o'er;
To feasting they went, with true merriment,
  And tippl'd strong liquor gillore.

Then Robin he took the pretty sweet babe,
  And cloth'd him from top to the toe
In garments of green, most gay to be seen,
  And gave him a curious long bow.

"Thou shalt be an archer as well as the best,
  And range in the greenwood with us;
Where we'll not want gold nor silver, behold,
  While bishops have ought in their purse.

"We live here like squires, or lords of renown,
  Without ere a foot of free land;
We feast on good cheer, with wine, ale and beer,
  And everything at our command."

Then musick and dancing did finish the day;
  At length, when the sun waxed low,
Then all the whole train thee grove did refrain,
  And unto their caves they did go.

And so ever after, as long as he liv'd,
  Although he was proper and tall,
Yet nevertheless, the truth to express,
  Still Little John they did him call.

Activity

This ballad is excellent for choral reading. There are many ways to orchestrate it. Here is one to try.

1. Read the ballad aloud in class; discuss the meanings of words which students do not know.

2. Remind students that a ballad is a song, so it should be read in rhythm.

3. Assign parts for the characters of Robin Hood, William Stutely, and Little John.

4. Divide the stanzas by counting from one to four and repeating until each stanza has a number from one to four.

5. Divide the class into four groups and number the groups from one to four. Each group's part is the stanzas with the same numbers.

6. Practice the "chorus" until everyone has it down pat, and perform it on a parents' night or for another class. Great fun!

The Diary

Another form of writing which was done by the educated person in the Elizabethan Age (and for some time after) was the diary. One of the most famous diaries available to us is probably *The Diary of Samuel Pepys* (pronounced "peeps"), which, while not written during this illustrious time, was written quite soon after.

Samuel Pepys began his diary in 1659 and continued writing it until his eyes became bad ten years or so later. One of the most interesting parts of the diary describes the Great Fire of London in 1666 and the actions and reactions of the citizens during that catastrophe.

Activity

Imagine yourself in one of the following positions and write a diary covering a period of one week from that person's perspective.

1. You are the young Edward, Prince of Wales, and Richard has had you put into the Tower of London. Write a diary of your first week in that terrible place. Include your feelings about Richard and what he has done.

2. You are Beatrice. Imagine the day when Benedick is coming home and reveal your real thoughts about him.

3. You are Juliet or Romeo. Describe your life before and during the five days covered by the play.

Note to teacher: You may wish to reproduce the pattern below for diary pages.

Date:

Dear Diary,

Questions for Discussion

Now that you have read plays and poetry by William Shakespeare, you may have questions about him or the characters in his works. Write any questions you have here. Discuss those questions and the ones below with your classmates.

1. *Romeo and Juliet*

   Why did Shakespeare have Romeo and Juliet die at the end of the play? Do you think the Montagues and the Capulets ever became friends? Why was Friar Lawrence so nosy and interfering? Do you think Nurse should have told Juliet's parents that Juliet and Romeo were going to get married? Did Nurse continue working for Juliet's family after Juliet was dead? Why was Romeo not arrested as soon as he had killed Tybalt? What do you think it was like to live in a place where there were no laws which applied to everyone (except for church laws)?

2. *Much Ado About Nothing*

   Did Beatrice and Benedick ever stop fighting after they were married? Did Claudio really believe that he was marrying a relative of Hero? Why did Don John go to so much trouble to make things bad for Claudio? What could Claudio ever have done to Don John to make him so revengeful? Do you believe anyone is all bad as Don John is shown to be? Do you believe anyone is as good as Hero? Was Dogberry stupid? In Kenneth Branagh's film of *Much Ado About Nothing*, Dogberry and the watch pretend to be riding horses when they go on and off the stage. Why do you think Branagh directed them to do that?

3. *Richard III*

   Can you think of any modern people who are as conniving and heartless as Richard? What is a person who has no conscience called? Why did the young princes go so willingly to the Tower? Do you think the Tower is haunted because of all the terrible things that have happened there? Was Richard crazy? Why did Lady Anne marry Richard after he had killed her husband? Why was Richard so desperate for a horse at the end of the play?

4. **Shakespeare**

   Does Shakespeare have any living descendants? Was it common in Shakespeare's time for 18-year-old men to marry women several years older than they were as he did? Why did Shakespeare's children have so few children of their own? How do you think Shakespeare learned so much about human nature living in a small town without television, movies, magazines, and newspapers? If Shakespeare were alive today, what do you believe he would think about the world today? Are the people in today's England as interested in history as Shakespeare and the people of his time were?

Shakespeare Scavenger Hunt

Within the pages of this unit, find the answers for the descriptions below. Circle the answers when you find them. Write the answers and the page numbers where you found them on the blank lines.

1. Name of Shakespeare's mother _____ _____

2. Maiden name of Shakespeare's wife _____ _____

3. Names of Shakespeare's three children _____ _____

4. Names of Shakespeare's two sons-in-law _____ _____

5. Two theaters in Shakespeare's London_____ _____

6. River running through London _____ _____

7. Infamous castle in London _____ _____

8. First play written by Shakespeare_____ _____

9. Eleventh play written by Shakespeare _____ _____

10. Item over an Elizabethan bed _____ _____

11. Item for storing clothing in a bedroom_____ _____

12. Two Elizabethan weapons _____ _____

13. Two Elizabethan musical instruments _____ _____

14. Name for a helmet _____ _____

15. Date of Shakespeare's birth _____ _____

16. Three characters in *Much Ado About Nothing* _____ _____

17. Instrument which looks like a piano_____ _____

18. Kind of roof on some English cottages _____ _____

19. Poem which tells a story_____ _____

20. One food Elizabethans did not know about _____ _____

21. Item which makes the air smell good_____ _____

Research Projects

Romeo and Juliet were two tragic characters Shakespeare chose to dramatize as star-crossed lovers who were victims of their society's view of the world. That their story is still loved is a tribute to the poet who was able to put flesh and blood on the bones of their story, so we can feel with them and experience with them their plight.

In *Richard III* Shakespeare showed us the plottings and manipulations of one who wanted power and was willing to do anything, even kill, to get what he wanted. It is a fascinating study of character, and we find ourselves mesmerized by this fiend who has no conscience.

Much Ado About Nothing gives us a silly story. If it ended differently, it would be a tragedy, but as it is, it is an enjoyable tale with Dogberry, the silliest of characters, and lovers who find everlasting joy together, despite their wrong-headed actions.

Many fascinating and often tragic people lived during the century in which Shakespeare wrote, including the mother and father of Queen Elizabeth I. Exploring the victories and tragedies of some of the real people, places, and events during this tremendously vigorous period can make the era come alive for us, and maybe even give us a better look at ourselves and our world in the process. Below are listed some suggestions for research projects your students might choose.

Suggested historical figures, places, and events to research:

❖ Sir Francis Drake
❖ The Spanish Armada
❖ John Hawkins
❖ Anne Boleyn
❖ Lady Jane Grey
❖ Privateers
❖ Jane Seymour
❖ Geoffrey Chaucer
❖ Edward VI
❖ London Bridge
❖ Eton School
❖ Cambridge University
❖ The Plague
❖ The Puritans
❖ Christ's Hospital, London

❖ Pieter Bruegel
❖ The Tower of London
❖ Witch hunting
❖ William Caxton and the printing press
❖ The Protestant Reformation
❖ The Gunpowder Plot
❖ Robert, Earl of Essex
❖ Saint Thomas à Becket
❖ Sir Walter Raleigh
❖ Mary, Queen of Scots
❖ Henry VIII
❖ Mary Tudor
❖ Anne of Cleves
❖ James I of England

❖ The Globe Theatre
❖ Stratford-upon-Avon
❖ Oxford University
❖ The spice trade
❖ Growth of the theater
❖ Sir Francis Bacon
❖ Rembrandt
❖ The hue and cry
❖ Newgate Prison
❖ The Tudors
❖ Sir Thomas More
❖ The Mary Rose
❖ Philip of Spain
❖ Pocahontas

Build an Elizabethan Museum

Museums are fascinating places full of all sorts of things. Inside a museum you might find clothing, utensils, jewelry, mummies, whole ships rebuilt which used to sail the seas, airplanes, automobiles, in fact everything which the people of an age used in all their living activities.

You can build your own Elizabethan museum in miniature on the insides of shoeboxes or other boxes of different sizes. In the pages of this book are many ideas for items to exhibit. You will find Elizabethan weapons, clothing, musical instruments, cottages, furniture, and many other things relating to the age of Shakespeare, all of them just waiting for you to make them in miniature.

Several students may want to do a museum as a group, with each of you taking one part, or one department, as your own special project. If this method is chosen, each student may wish to design a complete room (box) for a single display—a sailing ship model, a miniature model of Romeo dueling Tybalt, or a display of Elizabethan clothing. (There is no need, of course, for every room to be exactly the same size.) When all the projects are completed, you will have a museum of many rooms, richly supplied with illustrations and artifacts from the fascinating world of Shakespeare's England. You will have created what many great museums provide us with—a time machine to carry us to the past. Whether you work in a group, or build one by yourself, you will learn much about the items you choose to display.

Build your museum as a culminating project. Remember, you will be the curator of this museum. The curator is responsible for collecting and keeping track of the items displayed. Part of the job of being curator is keeping an up-to-date list of all the things in the museum and also making sure that the items are labeled correctly. When all "rooms" are completed, they should be arranged in some logical order (grouped by subject, perhaps) and then numbered. The last step for the curator is to prepare a catalogue for visitors that contains the list of items displayed and a directory of "rooms."

At parents' night, or during your culminating festival, your museum will be a very interesting part of the exhibits.

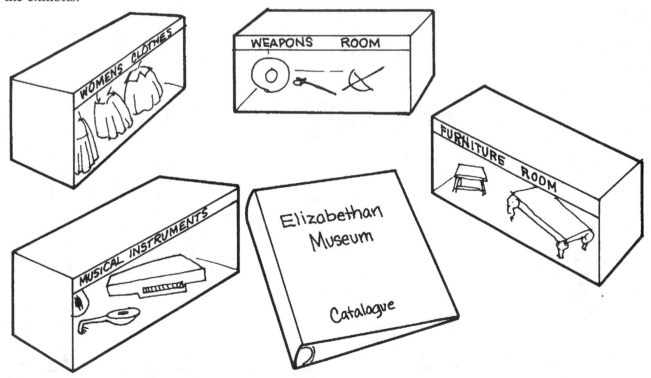

Build an Elizabethan Museum *(cont.)*

Elizabethan Furniture

Elizabethan furniture was made to serve the daily needs of sleeping, sitting, eating, and relaxing. Poor people were lucky to have a few of the daily necessities, but the families of the noblemen and the gentry were able to indulge their wishes for things which were more than just necessities. The furniture made during Shakespeare's time was much heavier and more solid-looking than most of the furniture we have today, and some of the pieces were heavily carved.

As you can see by the picture of a bedroom in a "great house" below, the furniture was square and rather massive. Beds were huge and usually included a paneled back, a canopy, large carved posts, and curtains which were closed at night. There was a practical reason for the canopy. The only sources of heat in the houses of the time were fireplaces. Although every room may have had a fireplace, England has a great deal of cold weather and rain, and it would have been cold during the night. The curtains around the bed helped hold in the body heat of the persons sleeping there.

The joint stool (used by most people as a place to sit) at the left of the picture was the most common piece of furniture. Only a few very important people would have had chairs with backs and arms. The carved chest was used for storing clothing and bedroom linens. Houses of the time did not have built-in closets or cabinets, and clothing needed to be stored until such time as it was needed. Only well-to-do families would have needed chests, however, because poor people probably would have had only one set of clothing, and that one not very good.

Utensils included kitchen items, different types of candleholders, and containers for drinks and food. The candleholder on the next page is one which would have held a kind of candle called a taper or a rushlight, which was made by dipping a rush into melted wax, which could be carried around from place to place. Leather bottles were used for carrying liquor. Other utensils included knives, shears for cutting cloth, stoneware drinking vessels and bottles and goblets.

Activity

In the bedroom section of your museum, place miniature furniture which you have made and which you have modeled after the furniture of Elizabethan times.

Build an Elizabethan Museum *(cont.)*

Elizabethan Furniture and Utensils

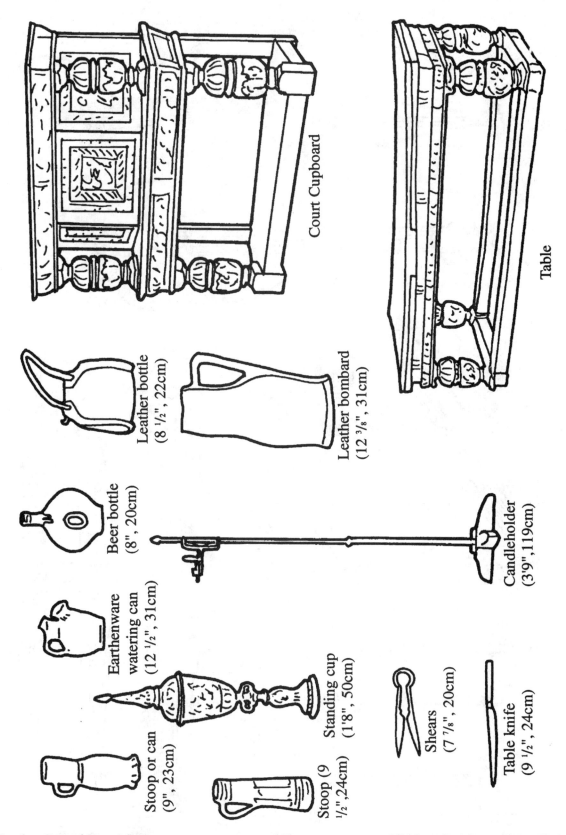

Court Cupboard

Table

Leather bottle (8 ½", 22cm)

Leather bombard (12 ³/₈", 31cm)

Beer bottle (8", 20cm)

Candleholder (3'9",119cm)

Earthenware watering can (12 ½", 31cm)

Standing cup (1'8", 50cm)

Shears (7 ⅞", 20cm)

Table knife (9 ½", 24cm)

Stoop or can (9", 23cm)

Stoop (9 ½",24cm)

Build an Elizabethan Museum *(cont.)*

Elizabethan Musical Instruments

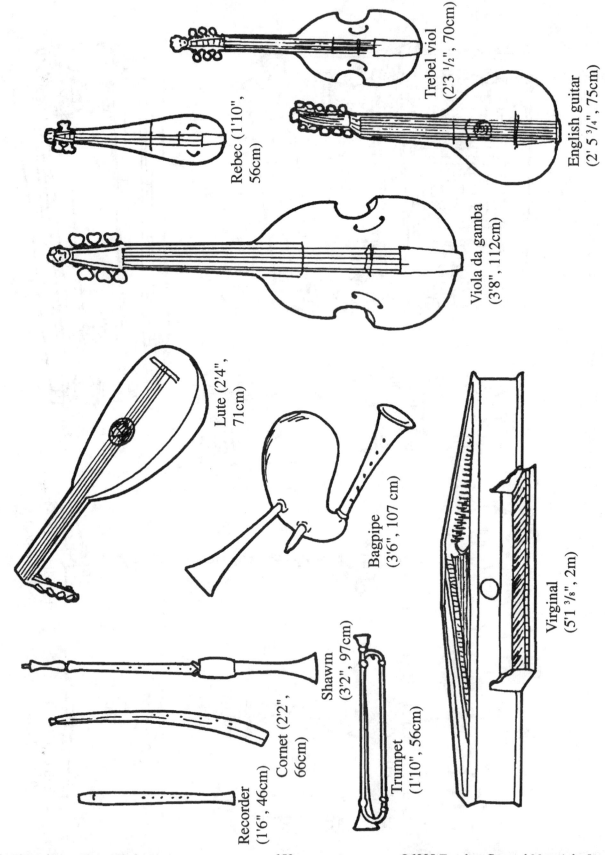

Trebel viol (2'3 ½", 70cm)

English guitar (2' 5 ¾", 75cm)

Rebec (1'10", 56cm)

Viola da gamba (3'8", 112cm)

Lute (2'4", 71cm)

Bagpipe (3'6", 107 cm)

Virginal (5'1 ⅜", 2m)

Shawm (3'2", 97cm)

Trumpet (1'10", 56cm)

Cornet (2'2", 66cm)

Recorder (1'6", 46cm)

Build an Elizabethan Museum *(cont.)*

Elizabethan Weapons

Most fighting that was done during Shakespeare's time was done hand to hand. Existing guns were not very accurate, so most weapons used were different types of swords, lances, knives, and poles. The weapons on the next page were the most common.

A *partisan* was used chiefly by palace guards. It was a heavy weapon and was used for close fighting in rooms and passages. The *halberd* was used for three kinds of fighting: the point for thrusting; the axehead for a smashing blow, the spike for thrusting scaling ladders or for pulling horsemen off their horses. The *bill* was used mainly by infantrymen and watchmen. The *hunting spear* was used when hunting boar (wild pigs).

The *crossbow* was a deadly weapon in the hands of an archer. It had a steel spring which was too powerful to be bent by hand, and it was set by winding up the handle until the string caught on the trigger. A *bird bow* was a small crossbow used for hunting birds.

There were several types of knives, swords, and daggers. The *sword* was the most popular English weapon until the *rapier* was invented in the sixteenth century. The sword was used mainly for cutting and thrusting. The *buckler* was used at the same time as the sword to protect the left hand when warding off the opponent's blows. Sometimes they were provided with a spike to thrust into the opponent's face. A *dagger* was carried in a sheath and used point upward in the left hand while one was fighting with a rapier in the right hand. The rapier was a long, light weapon with a thin blade of highly tempered steel. It was the fashionable weapon of Shakespeare's time, and it could be more than a match for the sword if someone used it well. There was also a *two-handed sword* which was just what its name suggests.

Most of the guns of the time were heavy, slow, and cumbersome to use in fighting. They took a lot of time to load. A charge of gunpowder first had to be poured in, then a ramrod was used to tamp the gunpowder down. Next a bullet was inserted, and some loose gunpowder was placed into a small pan beside the butt end of the barrel and lit. With the arquebus, the fighter would hold a lighted match to the touchhole at the base of the barrel instead, setting off the gunpowder by direct action. Whatever the way of setting off the gunpowder, if a line of troops set off their guns at once, they would be thickly enveloped in white gunsmoke.

The other weapons included the *dag*, which was a small pistol, and a *mace*, which was carried by horsemen for use in close combat. A miniature mace was carried by sergeants of the law as a badge of office.

Activity

Using the pictures on the next page, make models of these weapons to display in your museum.

Build an Elizabethan Museum *(cont.)*

Elizabethan Weapons

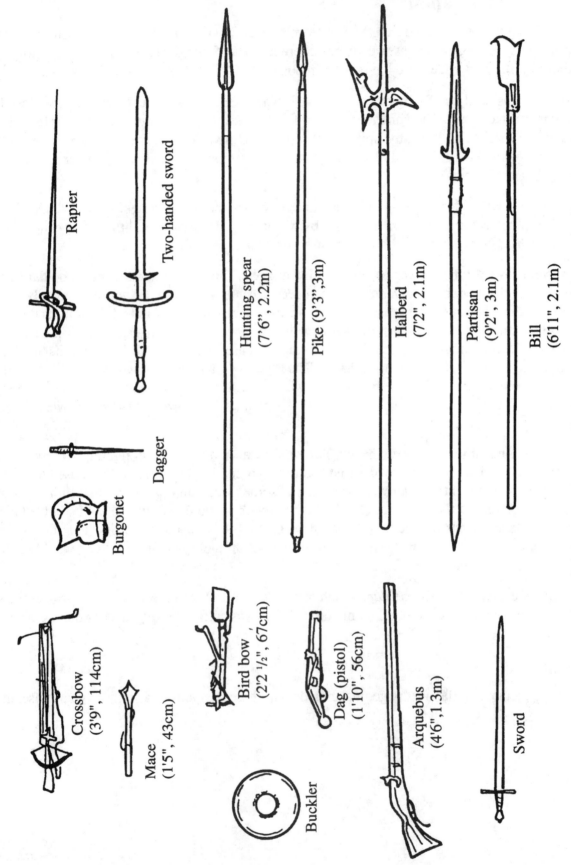

Rapier

Two-handed sword

Dagger

Burgonet

Hunting spear
(7'6", 2.2m)

Pike (9'3",3m)

Halberd
(7'2", 2.1m)

Partisan
(9'2", 3m)

Bill
(6'11", 2.1m)

Crossbow
(3'9", 114cm)

Mace
(1'5", 43cm)

Bird bow
(2'2 1/2", 67cm)

Dag (pistol)
(1'10", 56cm)

Buckler

Arquebus
(4'6",1.3m)

Sword

Produce a Shakespeare Play

Putting on a Shakespeare play of your own is not as hard as you think, and it can be a tremendous learning experience for your students. The key to success in your Shakespeare endeavor is to keep it simple. Remembering this will save you many worries and wasted moments. Here are some pieces of advice to make your planning easier.

Choose just the right play. Deciding which play, or plays, to produce is simply a matter of preference for teacher and students. Only you, as the teacher who knows the students in your particular class and their own mix of abilities, can make the decision. Will it be a comedy? Or will it be a tragedy? It can be one of the plays in this guide, or another of your choice. Getting past the hurdle of making this decision will get you far down the road to success. After you choose, you need only be concerned with the details. One note: If you are producing more than one play, achieve balance between them by, for example, doing one comedy and one drama. It will be more enjoyable and less confusing for students and audience alike.

Decide the length of the play. Some of the plays are much longer than others, so you may want to consider using a narrator to explain some of the action, thereby allowing you to cut some of the longer parts. You may even consider rewriting a play, but if you do, you will need to ensure somehow that new dialogue remains true in character to the original. Rewriting a play can, however, be a good learning experience in itself, so do not overlook the possibility.

Cast the characters. The number of students who will be participating will have much to do with determining which ones will play each character. Are you producing the play with only your class? Or are you working as a team with one or more other teachers and their classes? Whichever it is, allow each and every student to take a part, either in the play, in some other phase of the production, or both. Even children with reading problems or other disabilities can learn lines and play parts. Some will, of course, be able to learn more lines than others, in which case, shorter lines can be assigned to students unable to remember longer ones.

Set the stage. The actors of Shakespeare's day used little, if any, scenery, and many modern productions are produced on an almost totally bare stage. For many students, however, the excitement of being on a stage with certain properties can make the experience much more real, as well as provide an important job for the artistic students in your class. Here again, keep it simple. One way to do this is to use scenery frames. If you are producing two plays, the scenery for one play could be on one side and the scenery for the other play on the reverse side.

Produce a Shakespeare Play

(cont.)

Costume the actors. Although Shakespeare's plays are often played in modern dress or in styles other than Elizabethan dress, students usually enjoy being able to wear costumes. These do not need to be elaborate. To keep it simple, follow these guidelines. For boys: silky blouses with full, long sleeves, tights (black is best), vest, cape, and/or a tunic which can be held by a belt, and soft shoes such as ballet slippers or plain boots. For girls: long dresses and jewelry, especially beads and bracelets, and dressy shoes. Adding hip and shoulder pads can make the dresses look more Elizabethan.

Make it musical. Shakespeare included many songs in his plays, so consider adding audio effects with booming fanfares or mood pieces. See the bibliography for suggestions for music.

Use props. Properties, (called *props* for short), are the items used by the actors, things such as furniture, dishes, vases, and so forth, which the actors use on stage. When Shakespeare was producing his plays, very few properties were used, and the members of the audience had to use their imaginations as to what sorts of items were being used by the characters. Having some props, however, will add to the excitement, but again, keep it simple. Below are some props you may want to include in your production.

❖ Cover an old wooden chair with gold wrapping paper to use for a throne. Add "jewels" of old beads or crumpled pieces of colored foil paper.

❖ Make a crown for Richard from cardboard in the shape found on page 167.

❖ Use old goblets, dishes, etc., contributed by parents or other interested parties, painted gold.

❖ For the sword fight in *Romeo and Juliet*, make swords from heavy cardboard or pasteboard covered with foil.

❖ A folding cot can be used for the bier in *Romeo and Juliet* or for a bed. For different uses, just cover it with a different color spread which comes to the floor.

You can improvise any other props you want, and the students will enjoy making them.

Elizabethan Masque and Feast

You have just finished an extensive unit on Shakespeare, and it is appropriate for you to congratulate yourself and celebrate. What better way to do this than with an Elizabethan masque and feast which can be held in either your classroom or the multi-use room of your school. It can be as elaborate or as simple as you and your class decide to make it. Here are some hints to help you plan it.

It helps to delegate responsibilities for organizing the various activities. This is best done by dividing into committees to come up with ideas for specific events. The committees bring the ideas back to the class and make suggestions, and teacher and class decide together on exactly how to handle everything. Some committees might include these: display committee, dramatics committee, food committee, art committee, and (never to be overlooked) the clean-up committee.

Serving foods is a traditional way for people to celebrate, so on pages 158–159, you will find a sample menu and several typical dishes from England, which people there have served for many years. You may wish to substitute other dishes or simply have the students bring their lunches into the classroom and share the meal together. On page 164 is a scroll which may be reduced and used as invitations, or enlarged and used as placemats or as the background for displays.

Now is the time to show off all that the students have learned in this unit. Suggestions for displaying exhibits and demonstrating new skills are below.

Displays

❖ Plot plans of one of the stories
❖ Modern renditions of Elizabethan English
❖ Time lines of the history of the English language
❖ Pictures showing London during the period
❖ Sachets
❖ Sonnets written by the class
❖ Comparison charts of now and then
❖ Research projects
❖ Models or diagrams showing refrigeration
❖ Stick figures of people wearing Elizabethan clothing
❖ Time lines of the monarchs of England
❖ Pictures showing Elizabethan education
❖ Elizabethan half-masques
❖ Models or pictures of the Globe Theater
❖ Bar graphs showing results of Shakespeare surveys
❖ Invented words
❖ Dictionaries of Elizabethan words
❖ Comparisons of Elizabethan medicine and today's

Events

❖ Reader's theater production of a fable
❖ Oral presentations of spoken Old English
❖ Demonstrations of words descending from French
❖ Oral presentations of a news ballad
❖ Debate about the effectiveness of severe punishments
❖ Showing of Zeffirelli's *Romeo and Juliet*
❖ Having a homemade ice cream booth
❖ Dramatizations of scenes from the stories
❖ Presentation of Elizabethan music or dance
❖ Oral presentations of how the Elizabethans viewed the world
❖ Presentations of student-written Romeo and Juliet in modern English
❖ Elizabethan feast
❖ Demonstrations of how to read Shakespeare aloud
❖ Production of morality play

Elizabethan Masque and Feast *(cont.)*

A suggested menu would include any of the following:

- ❖ Cider
- ❖ Cheese
- ❖ Cheese Scones
- ❖ Roast Chicken
- ❖ Chicken Parcels
- ❖ Shepherd's Pie
- ❖ Jacket Potatoes with Fillings
- ❖ Courting Cake

Preparation of chicken or game hen:

From before Elizabethan times until the present, English meals have included various meats. Sometimes meats are roasted and served with Yorkshire pudding, gravy, and new potatoes in butter and fresh mint. Sometimes small amounts of meat are used with vegetables and/or pastry to make economical dishes such as shepherd's pie, steak and kidney pie, or pasties. Some dishes have interesting names like "Bubble and Squeak" or "Cook-a-leekie Soup". Any of these dishes could be used in addition to, or instead of, the ones for which recipes are included.

If cooking chicken or game hen, use these guidelines to determine your needs:

- ❖ 1 chicken (serves 3-4)
- ❖ 1 turkey leg (serves 1)
- ❖ 1 game hen (serves 2)

Recipes

Cheese and Chive Scones (Serves 10)

1 cup (250 g) self-rising flour
pinch salt
¼ cup (50 g) butter, diced
½ cup (125 g) grated cheddar cheese

1 tbsp. (15 mL) chopped fresh chives
½ cup (125 mL) milk plus extra for brushing

1. Sift flour into bowl.
2. Cut butter into flour until it is the consistency of corn meal.
3. Stir in half of cheese and all of chives.
4. Add milk and mix to form soft dough, then knead lightly until smooth.
5. Roll out on floured board to ½ in. (1.27 cm) thick. Cut into 10 rounds with biscuit cutter and brush tops with milk.
6. Place on baking sheet and bake at 450°F (230°C) for 7 to 10 minutes until golden brown.
7. Immediately sprinkle remaining cheese on tops and allow to melt before serving.

Courting Cake (Serves 12–16)

1 cup (250 g) butter or margarine
1 cup (250 g) sugar
4 eggs, beaten
1½ cup (350 g) self-rising flour

2–3 tbsp (30-45 mL) milk
10 fl. oz. (300 mL) whipping cream
1 cup (250 g) strawberries, sliced
confectioners sugar

1. Grease and flour three 7-inch (18 cm) round cake tins.
2. Cream butter and sugar together until pale and fluffy. Gradually add eggs, beating well after each addition. Fold in flour, and add just enough milk to give a soft dropping consistency.
3. Divide mixture evenly between the cake tins and bake at 375°F (190°C) for 25–30 minutes, until top springs back lightly when touched. Cool on wire racks.
4. Whip cream until it just holds its shape. Sandwich the layers together with the cream and berries, saving a few for decoration. Sprinkle top with confectioner's sugar and decorate with remaining berries.

Elizabethan Masque and Feast *(cont.)*

Jacket Potatoes with Fillings

Scrub potatoes and wrap in foil. Bake in 375°F (190°C) oven 1 hour or until potatoes feel soft when squeezed gently. For a microwave, scrub potatoes, prick 3 or 4 times with fork, and bake on high for 10 minutes until they feel soft when squeezed gently.

Fill with fillings of your choice, e.g., sour cream, butter, chives, cheese, chili beans, etc.

Shepherd's Pie (Serves four)

1 lb. (450 g) ground meat
1 large onion
1 bay leaf
2 oz. (50 g) sliced fresh mushrooms
2 carrots
$\frac{1}{8}$ cup (25 g) flour
1 cup (260 mL) beef stock

1 tbsp. (15 mL) tomato puree
salt and pepper to taste
1 $\frac{1}{2}$ lb. (700 g) potatoes, peeled and chopped
1 oz. (25 g) butter or margarine
4 tbsp. (60 mL) milk
$\frac{1}{4}$ cup (50 g) grated cheese

1. Crumble meat into skillet and stir over medium heat with next four ingredients 8 to 10 minutes.
2. Add flour and cook, stirring for 1 minute.
3. Add stock and puree and stir until the mixture thickens and boils.
4. Turn down heat and simmer gently for 25 minutes. Remove bay leaf and add salt and pepper to taste.
5. Spoon into 3 pint (1.7 liter) ovenproof dish.
6. Meanwhile, boil potatoes 20 minutes or until tender. Drain. Mash with milk and butter.
7. Pile mashed potatoes onto meat mixture and sprinkle with grated cheese.
8. Bake at 400°F (200°C) for 15–20 minutes. Serve hot.

Seafood Salad

Purchase enough seafood salad from the supermarket deli to serve the number of people to be present at your Elizabethan Masque and Feast. Arrange it attractively on a bed of fresh lettuce and decorate with olives and red and green bell peppers.

Chicken Parcels (Serves 4)

$\frac{1}{2}$ oz. (15 g) butter or margarine
1 small onion, washed, skinned and chopped
2 medium carrots, diced
1 tbsp. (15 mL) flour
1 tsp. (5 mL) mild curry powder
1 cup (250 mL) chicken stock

1 tsp. (5 mL) lemon juice
1 cup (250 g) boneless cooked chicken, chopped
Salt and pepper
13 oz. (368 g) packet frozen puff pastry, thawed
beaten egg for glaze

1. Melt butter in large sauce pan, add onion and carrots, cover and cook on medium heat for 4–5 minutes. Stir in flour and curry powder and cook, stirring, 1 minute. Remove from heat and gradually add stock.
2. Bring to boil, stirring; then simmer 2–3 minutes until thick.
3. Reduce heat and add lemon juice, chicken, salt and pepper. Allow to cool.
4. Roll out pastry dough on floured board and cut into 4 squares.
5. Place pastry on dampened baking sheets and spoon meat mixture onto pastry. Brush edges of pastry with water, and fold each square in half. Seal edges and crimp, then make 2 slashes on top of each parcel. Brush with egg.
6. Bake at 425°F (220°C) 15–20 minutes or until pastry is golden brown.

Festival of the Dramatic Arts and High Tea

After finishing a literature unit as comprehensive as this on Shakespeare, you have something to celebrate. And what better way could there be to celebrate these wonderful plays and poems by Shakespeare than by having a Festival of the Dramatic Arts and High Tea!

Your Festival can be simple or as elaborate as space, funds, and parent participation will allow. It can be as small as a classroom project, only for the students and teacher, or it can be a school-wide project involving other classrooms and several plays. However you choose to do it, it will be a great way to honor Shakespeare and to rejoice about all you have accomplished. Suggestions for foods you want to include are on page 161, and ideas for different displays and events are listed below. Other tips for making your festival a super celebration are these:

1. To begin your planning, divide into small brainstorming groups to come up with ideas for your festival.

2. Then, as a class, decide just what activities and displays you want your festival to include, who you would like to invite, and where you will hold the festival.

3. Choose committees to plan activities, foods, and clean up, and you are on your way to a great time!

Displays

- ❖ Maps of Shakespeare's London
- ❖ Pageants
- ❖ Illustrated dictionaries
- ❖ Slang dictionaries
- ❖ Stories using Shakespeare quotes
- ❖ Puppet stages
- ❖ Puppets
- ❖ Models of the Globe Theater
- ❖ Dioramas of scenes from plays
- ❖ Elizabethan poetry books
- ❖ Posters advertising *Much Ado About Nothing*
- ❖ Pictures of timber-framed houses
- ❖ Research projects
- ❖ Posters illustrating Shakespeare's world
- ❖ Charts illustrating how to convert Fahrenheit temperatures to Celsius
- ❖ Charts showing results of survey of obscure words in Shakespeare's works
- ❖ Response journals
- ❖ Letters to Hero
- ❖ Chart of chronology of Shakespeare plays
- ❖ Invite guests from drama department of local college to demonstrate Shakespearean drama

Events

- ❖ Production of one or more Shakespeare plays
- ❖ Morality play production
- ❖ Oral presentation about tragedy and comedy
- ❖ Demonstrations of optical illusions
- ❖ Oral presentations of stories using Shakespeare quotes
- ❖ Presentation of puppet plays
- ❖ Reader's theater of Shakespeare sonnets and other Elizabethan poetry
- ❖ Dramatizations of rewritten Shakespeare scenes
- ❖ Dramatizations of *Much Ado About Nothing* turned into tragedies
- ❖ Student impersonation of Shakespeare talking about one of his plays
- ❖ Oral presentation about Shakespeare and music
- ❖ Oral presentation of malapropisms
- ❖ Presentation by "tour guide" of Stratford-upon-Avon
- ❖ Recordings of Elizabethan music as background
- ❖ Cream tea in classroom "tea shop" featuring foods loved by English people
- ❖ Showing one or more films of Shakespeare's plays

Tea and Cakes

In Shakespeare's town of Stratford-upon-Avon is a delightful little tea room called Hathaway's Tea Shop in honor of Shakespeare's wife, Anne Hathaway. It is in one of the centuries-old timber-framed buildings for which the town is famous, and if you go upstairs to have tea, you must watch your step, because the old floors slant this way and that. Nonetheless, tea in Hathaway's is a wonderful experience as pretty young ladies in white aprons serve your tea and a variety of cakes.

The English love their tea and almost always drink it with cream or milk and sugar. An important part of the ceremony of having tea is that the milk or cream is poured into the cup first, and then the tea. Also remember that "cakes" in England are generally what Americans would call fancy cookies. "Biscuits" would be the plainer cookies or crackers. And at high tea, scones are always eaten with clotted or whipped cream and strawberry jam. Mmm—good! Try some of the suggestions below.

Sample Menu

Raisin scones with strawberry conserve
Assorted cookies and cakes
Cucumber and salmon sandwiches
Tea with cream or milk

Raisin Scones

1 cup (250 g) self-rising flour
pinch of salt
¼ cup (62 g) butter

½ cup (125 mL) raisins or currants
½ cup (125 mL) milk and extra for brushing

1. Heat oven to 450° F (230° C).
2. Put flour into bowl and cut in butter until mixture resembles bread crumbs. Stir in raisins.
3. Add milk and mix to form a soft dough; then knead quickly until smooth.
4. Roll out on floured bread board to ½ inch (1 cm) thick. Cut into rounds with a 2–inch (5 cm) cookie cutter.
5. Put rounds on baking sheets and brush tops with milk.
6. Bake 7–10 minutes until risen and golden.

Serve with strawberry conserve and whipped cream.

Cucumber and Salmon Sandwiches

White bread
Soft butter

English cucumber, sliced thinly
Canned salmon, flaked

1. Spread inside of bread with soft butter
2. Lay thinly sliced cucumber on buttered bread
3. Spread with flaked salmon and top with buttered bread. Cut into triangles and serve.

Strawberry Conserve

3 lb. (1.4 kg) fresh strawberries, hulled
3 lb. (1.4 kg) sugar

1. Layer strawberries in a large bowl with sugar. Cover and leave for 24 hours.
2. Put into large saucepan and bring to boil. Boil rapidly for 5 minutes, stirring.
3. Return mixture to bowl, cover, and leave in a cool place or refrigerator for 2 days.
4. Return to saucepan and again boil rapidly for 10 minutes. Cool for 15 minutes; then place in covered pot or jar as for jam.

Chronology of Shakespeare's Plays

Titus Andronicus, 1588–1594

The Comedy of Errors, 1588–1594

Henry VI, Part 1, 1590–1591

Henry VI, Part 2, 1590–1591

Henry VI, Part 3, 1590–1591

The Taming of the Shrew, 1590

Two Gentlemen of Verona, 1590–1595

King John, 1591

Richard III, 1592

Love's Labour's Lost, 1593

Romeo and Juliet, 1593–1596

A Midsummer Night's Dream, 1595–1596

The Merchant of Venice, 1596–1598

Richard II, 1595–1596

Henry VI, Part 1, 1596–1597

Henry VI, Part 2, 1597–1598

The Merry Wives of Windsor, 1597

Much Ado About Nothing, 1598

Henry V, 1599

Julius Caesar, 1599

As You Like It, 1600

Twelfth Night, 1599–1601

Hamlet, 1600

Troilus and Cressida, 1602

All's Well That Ends Well, 1602–1604

Measure for Measure, 1603–1604

Othello, 1604

King Lear, 1606

Macbeth, 1606

Timon of Athens, 1606

Anthony and Cleopatra, 1608

Coriolanus, 1609

Pericles, Prince of Tyre, 1607–1608
(possibly written with a collaborator)

Cymberline, 1609–1610

The Winter's Tale, 1610–1611

The Tempest, 1611

The Two Noble Kinsmen, 1613
(with John Fletcher)

Henry VIII, 1613
(with John Fletcher)

Bulletin Board Ideas

Bulletin boards using the following ideas can be made by either students or the teacher. The ideas suggested here are based on the principle that bulletin boards should be instructive and informative, as well as attractive, and should be considered teaching tools in the classroom or the school corridor. They can be fun to make at the same time and may be done as a cooperative effort between students and teacher.

The background of your bulletin board can add greatly to its effectiveness. A background of black butcher paper or construction paper is especially attractive and really highlights displays. Backgrounds may also be made of printed fabric (small mini–prints work well), wrapping paper, foil, or tissue paper. The scroll on page 164 may be enlarged to use as a background for displays. Some suggestions for displays:

❖ Display posters advertising the showing of the movie, *Romeo and Juliet,* planned by the class.

❖ Make a time line of royal monarchs in England about whom Shakespeare wrote dramas. Extend the time line to include events surrounding the discovery and colonization of North America.

❖ Construct a plot graph such as the one on page 37. Cut out words or letters from colored construction paper, or use markers to draw lines. Primary colors and turquoise with black are especially effective for a colorful display.

❖ Obtain pieces of fancy materials from home sewing boxes or fabric stores to make a chart of cut-out illustrations of Elizabethan clothing. Velvets, satins, and laces would be appropriate, as would ribbons. The same approach could be used to make a bulletin board or a scene from *Romeo and Juliet.*

❖ Make a time line showing the development of the English language from pre-Roman times through all the invasions until the present. Under each date list several examples of words coming from that source.

❖ Research Shakespeare's hometown, Stratford-upon-Avon, and make an illustrated relief picture of the town, showing the principal landmarks.

❖ Make a comparison chart of Old English weights and measures and the metric system of weights and measures.

❖ Display sonnets, news ballads, and other poems written by class members. Use Old English letters for headings and titles.

❖ Display bar graphs made of results of the Shakespeare surveys.

Scroll

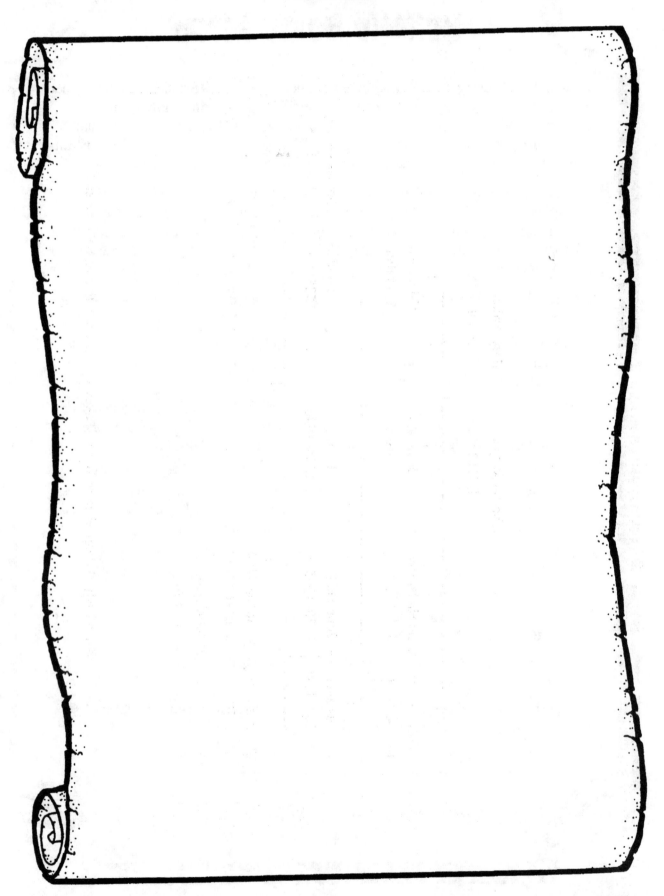

The Shakespeare Family Tree

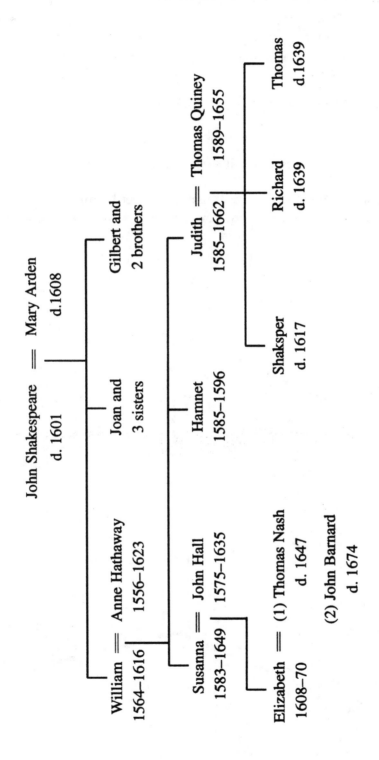

When Lady Barnard died in 1670, Shakespeare's direct line came to an end.

Scenery Frames

Scenery frames will serve you well for a long period of time and can be used in the production of any play simply by removing the student-made covers and replacing them with new ones. The scenery can also be stored for use at a later time by rolling up the sheets of fabric or painted butcher paper and putting them into storage, tubed to prevent damage. The frames may be folded flat and stored for use at another time for another play.

For each single frame you will need the following:

❖ 2 pieces 1" by 4" (2.5 cm by 10 cm) pine lumber 6 feet (2 m) long

❖ 2 pieces 1" by 4" (2.5 cm by 10 cm) pine lumber 4 feet (1.3 m) long

Assemble the lumber as shown and connect one frame to another by hinges. Two, three, or four frames may be connected and used as a folding screen. You may want to build one or more of each size.

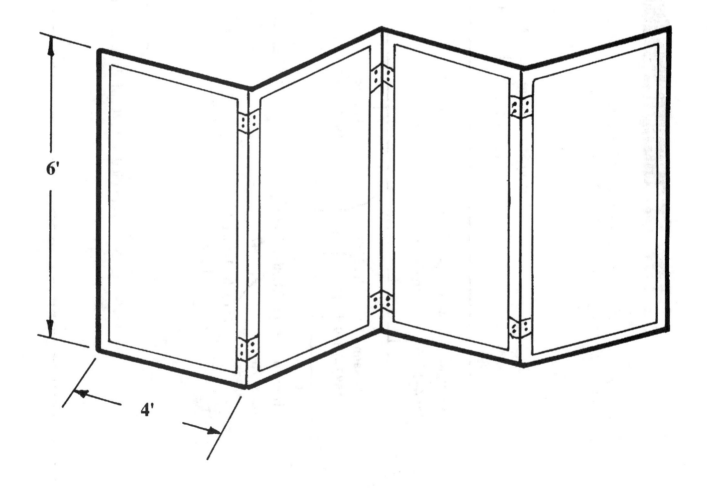

Crown Pattern

On a copy machine, enlarge this pattern about 135%; then fit it to size for the "king" in your play. Trace it onto pliable, lightweight cardboard, and cover it with gold foil, or paint it gold and put "jewels" on it.

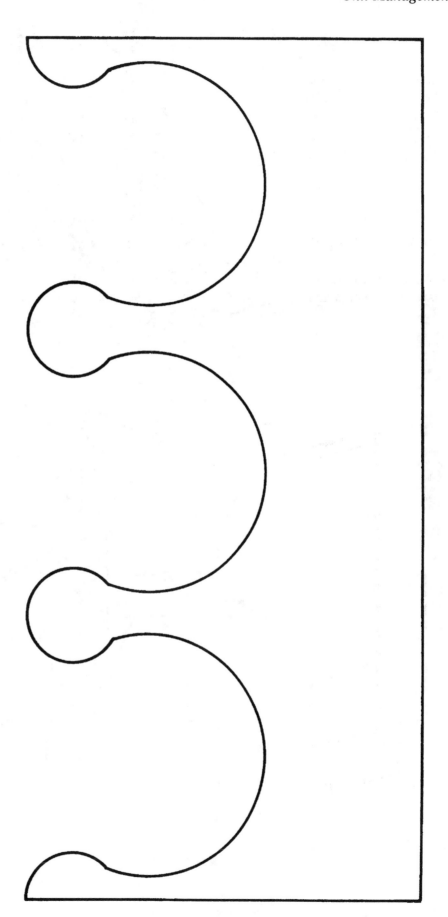

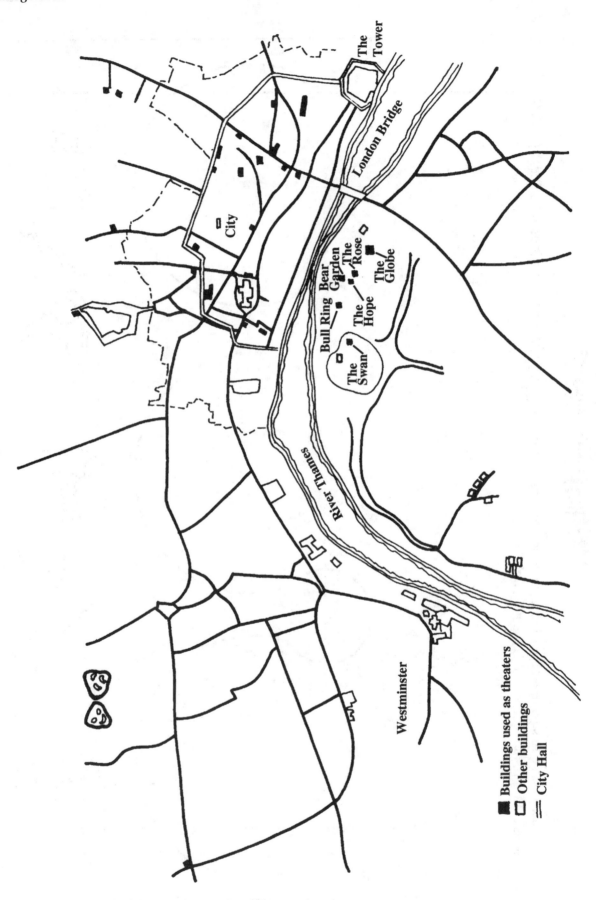

Theater Map of London

- The Tower
- London Bridge
- City
- The Rose
- The Globe
- Bear Garden
- The Hope
- Bull Ring
- The Swan
- River Thames
- Westminster

■ Buildings used as theaters
□ Other buildings
══ City Hall

Europe in 1560

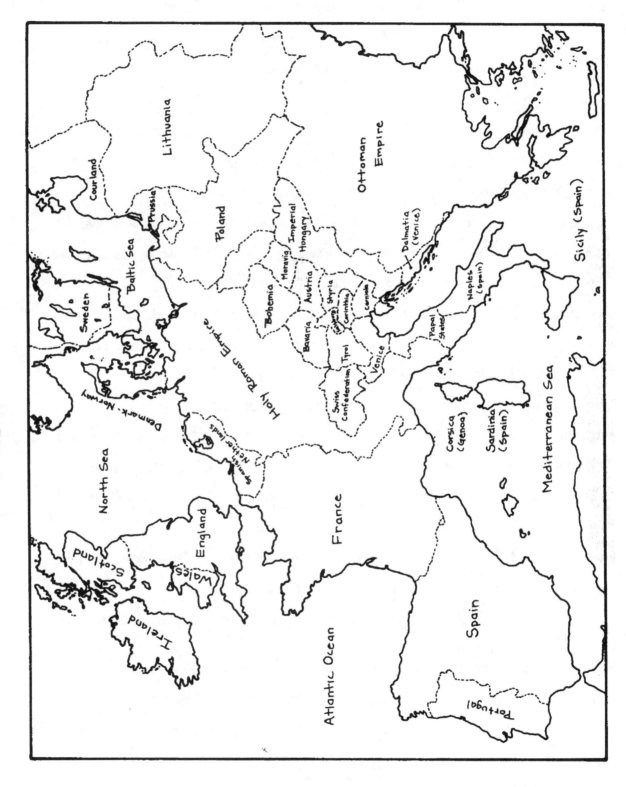

Bibliography

Fiction

Shakespeare, William. *Romeo and Juliet.* Washington Square Press, 1992.

_____. *Romeo and Juliet.* Abridged by Leon Garfield, Alfred A Knopf, 1992.

Twain, Mark. *The Prince and the Pauper.* Dell Publishing, 1985.

Resources

Ayto, John. *Dictionary of Word Origins.* Arcade Publishing, Little, Brown and Company, 1990.

Bartlett, John. *Familiar Quotations.* Little, Brown and Company, 1955.

Birch, Beverly. *Shakespeare's Stories.* Peter Bedrick Books, 1988.

Birt, David. *Plague and Fire.* Longman Group Limited Resources Unit. Great Britain, 1976.

Brown, John Russell. *Shakespeare and His Theater.* Lothrop, Lee & Shepard Books, 1982.

Burrell, Roy. *The Tudors and the Stuarts.* Oxford University Press, 1980.

Butterfield, Moira. *The Usborne Book of London.* Usborne Publishing Ltd., London, 1987.

Chute, Marchette. *An Introduction to Shakespeare.* Scholastic Inc., E.P. Dutton and Company, 1979.

Consumer Guide, editors. *The Big Book of How Things Work.* Publications International, LTD., 1991.

Epstein, Norrie. *The Friendly Shakespeare.* Viking Penguin, 1993.

Freeman, John and Sharpe Sue. *This Beautiful City London.* Bison Books Ltd., London, 1986.

Frye, Roland Mushat. *Shakespeare's Life and Times.* Princeton University Press, 1967.

Grun, Bernard. *The Timetables of History.* Simon & Schuster, 1975.

Halliday, F.E. *Shakespeare and His World.* Charles Scribner's Sons, 1979.

Harrison, G.B., Editor. *Shakespeare: the Complete Works.* Harcourt, Brace & World, 1968.

Holland, Clive. *Things Seen in Shakespeare's Country.* Seely, Service & Co. Limited, London, No date.

Horizon Magazine. *Shakespeare's England.* Harper & Row, 1964 by American Heritage Co., Inc., New York.

Kay, Dennis. *Shakespeare: His Life, Work, and Era.* Quill William Morrow, 1992.

Lamb, Charles and Mary. *Tales from Shakespeare.* Weathervane Books, 1975.

_____. *Tales from Shakespeare.* Macmillan Publishing Co., Inc., 1963.

Lepsky, Ibi. *William Shakespeare.* Barron's, New York, Toronto, 1988.

Miles, Bernard. *Favorite Tales From Shakespeare.* Hamlyn Publishing Group Limited, London, 1976.

Milk Marketing Board. *The Dairy Book of British Food.* Ebury Press, London, 1988.

Bibliography (cont.)

Pepys, Samuel. *The Diary of Samuel Pepys.* Collins Clear-Type Press, London and Glasgow, 1825.

Price, George R.. *Reading Shakespeare's Plays.* Barrons Educational Series, 1962.

O'Scanlon, Patricia and Judith Kennedy. "Guide to the Green Show." Oregon Shakespeare Festival, 1992.

The Random House Children's Encyclopedia. Random House, 1991.

Schoenbaum, S. *William Shakespeare: A Compact Documentary Life.* Oxford University Press, 1977.

_____ *Shakespeare, The Globe and the World.* Oxford University Press, Oxford, 1979.

Smith, Lacey Baldwin. *The Elizabethan World.* Houghton Mifflin Company, 1991.

Speed, Peter and Mary. *Farmers and Townsfolk, The Elizabethan Age.* Oxford University Press, Oxford, 1987.

Speed, Peter and Mary. *The Queen, Nobles, and Gentry, The Elizabethan Age.* Oxford University Press, Oxford, 1987.

_____. *The Seamen, The Elizabethan Age.* Oxford University Press, Oxford, 1987.

Stanley, Diane and Peter Vennema. *The Bard of Avon.* Morrow Junior Books, 1992.

Turner, Dorothy. *Great Lives Series: William Shakespeare.* Bookwright Press, 1985.

Virgoe, Roger, Editor. *Private Life in the Fifteenth Century, Illustrated Letters of the Paston Family.* Weidenfeld and Nicolson, 1989.

Tapes

Ball, Patrick and Drasin, Daniel. *Celtic Harp Volume Two,* (Haunting and lyrical folk music of the British Isles as played on the celtic harp). Fortuna Records, Novato, California, 1983.

(The following tapes are available through the Tudor Guild, Oregon Shakespeare Festival, 15. S. Pioneer, Ashland, Oregon, 97520)

Actors of the Oregon Shakespeare Festival, *Selected Sonnets of William Shakespeare,* Oregon Shakespeare Festival, Ashland, Oregon, 1990.

Kennedy, Judith. *Popular Dances of the Renaissance, Dance Music with Instructions,* Oregon Shakespeare Festival, 1985.

Musicians of the Oregon Shakespeare Festival, *Terra Nova Consort, Somewhat Musing,* Freeman Studios, Ashland, Oregon.

Videos, Movies

Hamlet, Warner Bros., Directed by Franco Zeffirelli with Mel Gibson.

Henry V, Majestic Films International, Directed by Kenneth Branagh, 1989.

Bibliography *(cont.)*

Videos, Movies *(cont.)*

Julius Caesar, Ambrose Video, produced by BBC/Time-Life.

Othello, Ambrose Video Publishing, Produced by BBC/Time-Life Films, 1982.

Romeo and Juliet, Produced by Zeffirelli. The one film treatment of the play in which teenagers play the roles, rather than older actors and actresses: outstanding, but teacher must view first because of adult scenes, 1968.

West Side Story, starring Natalie Wood as Maria in musical with modern urban setting, composed by Leonard Bernstein and based on plot of *Romeo and Juliet.*

The following video tapes are available from Random House Home Videos, Random House, Inc., 400 Hahn Rd., Westminter, Maryland, 21157, Phone 1–800–726–0600:

Hamlet

A Midsummer Night's Dream

The Tempest

Twelfth Night

Romeo and Juliet

Macbeth

Special thanks to Frank G. Nigro of Vanderbilt University for his treatment of Shakespearean sonnets in personal correspondence, June 20, 1993.

Answer Key

Page 25

It happened that season that on a day
In Southwark, at The Tabard, as I lay
Ready to go on my pilgrimage to
Canterbury, with a full devout heart,
At night there came into that hostelry
Some nine and twenty in a company
Of sundry folk by chance falling
Into fellowship, and they were pilgrims all,
That towards Canterbury meant to ride.
The rooms and stables of the the inn were wide;
They made us easy, all was of the best.
And shortly, when the sun had gone to rest,
Since I had spoken to every one of them,
I soon was one of them in fellowship
And made forward to rise early and take our way
To Canterbury, as I told you before.
But nonetheless, while I have time and space,
Before my story takes further pace,
I think it according to reason (reasonable)
To tell you the condition
Of each of them, as it seemed to me,
Of which they were and of what degree,
And also in what array they were in;
And at a Knight then I will first begin.

Page 34

1. 1 ft; 33.3 cm
2. 1.5 ft; .5 meter
3. 10 in; 27 cm
4. 1.75 ft. or 21 in; 58.3 cm
5. 6.2 in; 16.5 cm
10. 6 ft; 2 meters

Page 35

1. props
2. stage
3. audience
4. director
5. set
6. history
7. lines
8. tragedy
9. narrator
10. playwright
11. leading man, or male lead
12. ingenue or leading lady
13. London, England
14. action
15. comedy
16. script
17. curtain
18. cast
19. wings
20. applause

Page 44

1. The Capulets and Montaques are in a fight together which is a running feud between the two families.
2. Part of Romeo's speech of love as he looks up the balcony at Juliet.
3. Juliet's nurse thinks Juliet is dead.
4. Romeo says this to the Friar to get poison, so he can kill himself.
5. Juliet says this about her love for Romeo.
6. The Friar says this to Romeo and Juliet when he is about to marry them.

Page 45

Matching

1. G
2. F
3. I
4. E
5. C
6. A
7. J
8. H
9. D
10. B

True or False

1. False
2. True
3. True

Answer Key *(cont.)*

Page 45 *(cont.)*

4. False
5. True

Short Answers

1. Nurse, Friar Lawrence.
2. There was a big fight between the Montagues and the Capulets.
3. At a balcony.
4. He thought Juliet was dead.
5. Friar Lawrence.

Essay: Accept all appropriate responses.

Page 57

1. 8 x 9 = 72 yards (meters)
2. 10.27 yards (meters)
3. $174.46
4. $201.50
5. $208.37
6. $558.00, per week
   $29,016 per year
7. 45
8. $1150.13
9. $999.50
10. $591.20

Page 62

1. Beatrice telling Benedick she doesn't like him.
2. Benedick telling Beatrice he doesn't like her.
3. Claudio is in love with Hero.
4. Don John telling that he wants to mess up Claudio.
5. Beatrice describing Don John.
6. Don Pedro telling Claudio he has interceeded for him with Hero.
7. Song sung by Balthasar.
8. The three women speak in Beatrice's earshot that Benedick is in love with her.
9. Don John tells Claudio that Hero is unfaithful.
10. Dogberry speaking with words he does not understand, so people are confused when they hear him.

11. Claudio repudiates Hero at what was to be their wedding.
12. Leonato tells Claudio that because of his wronging of Hero, she is dead.
13. Benedick telling Beatrice he doesn't want to love her.
14. Claudio is tricked into marrying Hero, when he thinks she is dead.
15. Benedick tells Beatrice to be quiet and kisses her.

Page 63

Matching

1. D
2. E
3. K
4. H
5. L
6. G
7. B
8. J
9. A
10. F
11. C
12. I

True or False

1. True
2. False
3. False
4. False
5. False

Short Answer

1. Don John
2. He talked too much, he's a bad hunter, he eats too much, among other complaints.
3. Allowed herself to be used by Borachio to hurt Hero.
4. Messina
5. He feels she has been slandered and that she is really virtuous.

Answer Key *(cont.)*

Essay

Accept answers which include the following: love at first sight; a parent's love for a child; love covered up by insults; friendship, etc.

Page 90

1. The beginning of Richard's opening soliloquy in which he describes how he is going to become king of England.
2. Richard thinks of how he will kill Clarence, even when he is pretending to be Clarence's friend.
3. Richard plans to marry the dead man's wife and kill her later.
4. The ghost of Margaret tells what she knows about Richard.
5. One of the murderers talking about conscience and how it prevents a man from doing what he knows he should not do.
6. Richard plans to kill the little princes.
7. Tyrrel tells that the princes have been killed.
8. Buckingham, Richard's supposed friend, goes to be beheaded.
9. From Richmond's oration to his soldiers as they prepare to defeat Richard.
10. Richard has been defeated and his horse killed.

Page 91

Matching

1. C
2. D
3. F
4. G
5. H or J
6. J or H
7. I
8. E
9. B
10. A

True or False

1. True
2. False
3. False
4. True
5. False

Short Answer

1. England
2. A horse
3. Get rid of her after he has used her; kill her
4. Accept any description which fits the Tower of London
5. Anne, Clarence, Edward VI, the two young princes, Buckingham among others

Essay: Accept all appropriate responses.

Page 96

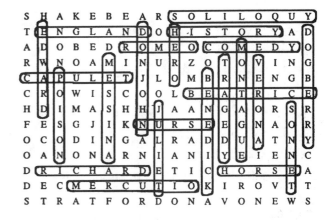

Page 98

Page 102

Answers given are approximate.

1. 8 liters
2. 2,500 millimeters or 2.5 liters
3. 3,750 millimeters or 3.75 liters
4. 45 millimeters
5. 125 millimeters
6. 75 millimeters
7. 1,750 millimeters or 1.75 liters
8. 375 millimeters
9. 4 liters
10. 1,440 grams or 1.44 kilogram
11. 120 grams
12. 960,000 grams or 960 kilograms
13. 30 centimeters
14. 15 centimeters
15. 90 centimeters

Page 103

1. 2,444 general admission
2. 1,645/5,687 = 28.9%
3. 1,598/5,687 = 28.1%
4. 1,645 x 2.57 = 4,227 seniors in April.
5. 4,258/1,598 = 266%
6. 11,977 total
7. 12,000 – 5,687 = 6,313 ticket increase; 111%
8. .58 x 1645 = 954 seniors; 927 juniors; 1,418 general admission
9. 1,395 x $2.50 = $3,487.50 total; $3,173.63 profit
10. $1.16 on each soda; $116.00 on 100 sodas; $686.72 on 592 sodas; $1.16/$1.50 = 77.3% profit

Page 106

1. All diseases: 1, July: 2, August; 3, September. The plague: 1, August; 2, July; 3, September
2. 11,503/25,886 = 44.4%
3. 25,886/250,000 = 10.3% from various diseases; 11,503/250,000 = 4.6% from plague
4. Varies with size of class. In a class of 30, three would have died of various diseases; 1.38, or between one and two students would have died of the plague.
5. 100 per thousand
6. 2,880 of the plague; 6093 of various diseases; plague deaths = 47.2% of all diseases.
7. 2,930 deaths from the plague; 5,948 of all diseases; plague deaths = 49.2% of deaths from various diseases.
8. Months are warmer; people out among each other, etc. Accept appropriate responses.

Page 107

°C	°F
30	86
23	73.4
18	64.4
27	80.6
8	46.4
4	39.2
41	105.8
15	59
45	113

Page 147

1. Mary Arden
2. Anne Hathaway
3. Susanna, Judith, Hamnet
4. John Hall, Thomas Quiney
5. Swan, Globe, The Theater, The Rose
6. The Thames
7. Tower of London
8. *Titus Andronicus*
9. *Romeo and Juliet*
10. Canopy
11. Chest
12. Accept any from chart
13. Accept any from chart
14. Burgonet
15. 1564
16. Accept any correct answers
17. Verginal
18. Thatched
19. Ballad
20. Tomatoes, hamburgers, etc.
21. Sachet